Oxstalls Library
University of Gloucestershire
Oxstalls Campus, Oxstalls Lane
Longlevens, Gloucester
Gloucestershire
GL2 9HW

ABOUT THE AUTHOR

Peter Bolt is a management consultant, mentor, coach and business strategist. He founded The Bolt Consultancy in 1988 and his client list includes notable blue-chip companies as well as various organisations of different shapes and sizes.

He spent many years with Unilever in the UK and overseas, and considers the time spent as a graduate trainee vital to his success. He then worked for HP Bulmer before being appointed Consultant Director with Marketing Solutions Ltd. in the early 1980s.

Peter has presented several public lectures and seminars, including his "Masterclass in Management" at the Institute of Directors, as well as in-house with numerous companies and local authorities. He is a member of the Institute of Directors, the Marketing Society and the Professional Speakers' Association.

He is married, with a film producer son and an actress daughter. He and his wife divide their time between London and Herefordshire.

THE WHOLE MANAGER

*Achieving Success Without
Selling Your Soul*

Peter Bolt

Oak Tree Press
Dublin

Oak Tree Press
Merrion Building
Lower Merrion Street
Dublin 2, Ireland
www.oaktreepress.com

A catalogue record of this book is
available from the British Library.

ISBN 1 86076 133 X

Printed in Britain by MPG Books
Bodmin, Cornwall

CONTENTS

ACKNOWLEDGEMENTS

There are many people who have helped to make this book a reality. Their encouragement goes back a long way and it is good to have a chance to thank them.

Firstly, my family, Sue, Jeremy and Anna, who have been a tower of strength in so many ways. Indeed, my wife Sue has been my nugget of gold all along.

Andrew King, in particular, and Peter Humphrey, Ronnie McCrum, Chris Locke, Michael Colborne, Chris Beale, Olaf Willoughby and Rob Coates have all given valuable advice on many occasions. I'd also like to thank Tack International, the training organisation, who sponsored my "Masterclass in Management" which was the forerunner to this book.

There are four clients with whom I have worked since the early 1980s. We have had numerous discussions on management which have proved invaluable to me. So special thanks to Tim Green, Managing Director, Shell Bitumen; David Clayton-Smith, Customer Marketing Director, Boots; Nick Holmes, Managing Director, Interbrew UK; and Mark Fairchild, Vice President, BancTec.

David Givens of Oak Tree Press has been very patient and helpful in all his advice, and also a meticulous editor.

I thank you all and also my many friends and clients who have put up with my passion for management for so long. You are all part of this.

PREFACE

In over thirty years of management experience and consulting I have frequently come across very talented people, people who absolutely excel at their work, who are then promoted to a management position and don't have a clue what to do next. Their technical skills might be superb, they might be very capable in general, but they have no idea how to manage other people, how to be prioritised and manage their time well, how to manage their boss — indeed, how to manage themselves. This book should be of help to them, as well as to managers higher up the ladder.

The truth is that very few managers are ever actually taught how to manage. They may have taken courses in various management skills, but in general they are left to get on with it, to sink or swim. In particular, they are never taught the *practical* things that can make the difference between success or failure in the workplace. And even worse, no one ever tells them how to balance their work life and home life, how to be a success on the job *and* in their personal lives.

This book is very much about managing yourself in all kinds of situations. Its focus is on practical tips and techniques that will help you to get the most out of yourself. Readers looking for complicated management theory and statistical analysis should go elsewhere. This book is based on a series of "Masterclass in Management" seminars given to numerous public and in-house audiences over the years, as well as hundreds of management consulting and executive coaching assignments. It is a no-nonsense, hands-on guide to the realities of management.

The response I've received to the lectures and one-to-one mentoring sessions has been extremely enthusiastic and very gratifying, and eventually convinced me to put my thoughts down on paper. There seems to be a palpable sense of relief as people realise that they can be a successful manager and still have a life, that they can rise to the top without being underhanded and duplicitous, that they can achieve success without selling their soul. It's as if the floodgates have opened and people realise there is another way.

It is hoped that this book will resonate with women as well as men. One of the central themes of the book — how to be a success at work and at home — is one that women have been grappling with for years as they try to combine the pressures of work with responsibilities at home. Many of the experiences recounted in the following pages are likely to sound quite familiar to women, although men are increasingly struggling with the difficulty of finding the balance between work and home.

In the 1970s I was diagnosed with a serious illness and told that I should get my affairs in order. It was at that point that I realised that time is our most precious possession and that life is for living. Since then I have been fascinated by the idea of how to achieve success without sacrificing your integrity, your home life or your self-respect. I hope that the advice and experiences contained in the following pages help you on your way to becoming a successful Whole Manager. Good luck.

Peter Bolt
Chiswick, London
April 1999

Chapter One

MANAGING YOURSELF

If You Can't Manage Yourself . . .

We begin with a basic question: How can you possibly hope to manage your unit, team, organisation or company if you can't manage yourself? That is, how can you help others to be focused on the job at hand, to be prioritised and well prepared at all times, if you don't meet such basic requirements yourself? The sad fact is that many managers are not good at managing themselves, and in this chapter — indeed, throughout the book — we will look at some positive actions and approaches that will help you to get the most out of yourself. Often the problem is simply one of not realising the need to take action, followed by not knowing exactly how to go about it.

In my consultancy work I often meet with clients who are operating considerably below their potential — I would estimate in some cases as much as 20–30 per cent below their true capability. As I discuss with them the possible reasons for their under-performance, the same issues invariably arise: they are not prioritised and not planning ahead; they are reactive rather than proactive; they are slaves of time. This chapter will address these and other common failings that may be preventing you from achieving success.

Part of the problem is that managers are seldom, if ever, taught *how* to manage, and in particular how to manage themselves. Management is an art, but it is one that needs to be worked at all the time. Among the topics to be addressed in this chapter that will help you become a more effective manager are the importance of preparation; why you should welcome accountability; managing with "bottle"; developing a positive attitude; making the most of adversity; and finally, the key issue of how to manage the way you are perceived by others.

The critical issue of managing your time will be dealt with in detail in the following chapter.

Preparation is the Key

Have you heard of the six P's? *Poor preparation produces piddling poor performance.* Most managers appreciate a certain need for preparation but don't give it nearly as much attention as it deserves. Think about the preparation of professional athletes. A famous golfer once chipped out of a bunker straight into the hole and overheard a spectator claim that he had just been "lucky", to which his reply was, "That may be so, but the more I practise the luckier I get."

What's true for professional sportsmen and athletes is equally true for managers. The more you prepare (practise) the luckier you will get. In fact, I would say that in business and in life one could define "luck" as "preparation plus opportunity". In other words, you can take positive steps that will influence your luck.

I have a client who fully understands the necessity of preparation, particularly for matters of importance. For example, if he has a very important presentation scheduled eight weeks ahead, he would mark his diary as follows:

D-Day minus 56	Skeleton Approach
D-Day minus 44	First Draft
D-Day minus 32	Second Draft
D-Day minus 24	Third Draft
D-Day minus 17	Fourth Draft
D-Day minus 10	Final Draft
D-Day minus 8	Rehearsal
D-Day minus 5	Rehearsal
D-day minus 3	Final Dress Rehearsal

He places those milestones in his diary, as well as on a separate sheet showing the critical path for this project, noting all the actions that he and others must take from day one through to the day of presentation. It covers every single point, including all the questions that are likely to be asked at the presentation itself. Thus, eight weeks before the event, he has begun the preparation and scheduled in his diary adequate time to give the project the attention it needs.

Why is such preparation important? Like the golfer who spends hours practising a particular shot so as to be able to execute it to perfection in competition, you need to practise *your* craft so that you can perform it effortlessly on the day. You need exactly the same kind of mindset to achieve excellence. And note that it doesn't necessarily mean working into the late hours of the night to accomplish it — it means that you need to think ahead and be prioritised (for tips on time management, see Chapter 2).

Another reason that such an approach to preparation is vital is that it will give you considerable self-confidence right from the start. You will *know* that you are prepared and that your brain is fully engaged — even your subconscious will kick into gear between times, which will enhance the quality of thinking, the clarity of writing and even the anticipation of any questions or objections to your proposal. Believe me: preparation is key.

Accountability

To get the best out of yourself you need to feel accountable for your actions and for those of your team. Basically, that means not leaning on others for help and not looking for excuses when things go wrong. Only by adopting a mindset of full responsibility will you be able to make the most of your talents.

A manager I worked with in a large blue-chip company once told me that he was not really accountable for his performance and that the boundaries of his job were unclear. He felt that neither success nor failure could be identified and, not surprisingly, he was frustrated and de-motivated. We discussed the situation, realised that it could not continue, and decided to act. He went to his boss and managed to agree with him a clear job description and a set of standards on which he would be judged. His performance and attitude improved immediately.

Even in organisations that have detailed annual appraisal procedures — which I personally feel are not always very effective — it is important for managers to understand what measurement factors are in place for them and to have discussions with their boss every few months or so to check on their progress. In that way they will feel truly accountable.

Managing with "Bottle"

> **Bottle** — noun (Brit. Informal): "the courage or confidence to do something difficult" (*The New Oxford Dictionary of English*)

> **Bottle** — noun (Brit. Slang): "courage, nerve, initiative" (*Collins Concise English Dictionary*)

When I observe managers and directors who continually achieve success there is often a certain characteristic — a mixture of firmness, strength of character, courage, integrity, and being true to oneself — that I call "bottle". To remind me of how essential this quality is I keep a fine nineteenth-century glass ale bottle on my desk. To explain the significance of "bottle", I'll give two examples.

A senior manager of a mid-sized company was asked to prepare a paper on an important project that the board was keen to develop. He had an ideal member on his team who could write the report and gave her a clear briefing on it.

When the report was produced, it was of very high quality and the senior manager presented it to the board, who were duly impressed. The question then arose, however, of who should get credit for the report. Should the senior manager just present it to the board as if it came from him personally, or should he fully acknowledge that his staff member had actually prepared it and should receive the accolades?

The second option is obviously the one with "bottle". If the manager had chosen the first option and implied that the paper was his own, the staff member would have become aware of it (they always do) and been demotivated. The board most likely would have realised that the writing was a bit different from the senior manager's usual style, suspect that someone else had actually written it, and think less highly of him for passing it off as his own. And the senior manager himself would have known that he was being less than fair with his staff member. Demotivation all around.

On the other hand, by taking the "bottle" option and passing credit to where it was due, the staff member would have felt acknowledged and motivated, the board would have been impressed that the senior manager had a good team and delegated well, and the manager himself would know that he had done the right thing.

Another example involves one of my clients who was on the board of a blue-chip company. The company had received an in-depth recommendation from one of the top management consultancies concerning the reorganisation of a particular department that was of considerable importance to the company. The main board had accepted the recommendations, but my client, who was a "lesser" board member, felt strongly that the change was a bad idea and would jeopardise the company's future. He decided to take a stand. At an important follow-up meeting, he stood up and made his case before 20 influential executives in the company. Initially, there was considerable consternation that my client wasn't going along with the recommendations, but he felt strongly about the issue and stood his ground. He restated his objections and eventually was able to convince the group that he was right. This took considerable courage, clear-mindedness, strength of character and personal self-belief. He decided that this particular battle was worth fighting — and please note that that *isn't* always the case — and went on to considerable success with the company.

Throughout your career you will have many opportunities to show your "bottle". By making the right choices — ones that show your courage and integrity — you will grow and mature as a manager and as a person. Think seriously about this — and maybe get your own bottle to put on your desk as a reminder!

Developing a Positive Attitude

Building on the "bottle" factor, it is worth noting the importance in general of having a positive attitude about your abilities. Such attitudes seem to come naturally to people in the US, New Zealand and elsewhere, but less so in the UK.

In New Zealand, for example, if someone discusses a new opportunity or initiative, the response is likely to be one of enthusiasm with suggestions on how to remove whatever barrier stands in the way. In the US the acronym GOYA — get off your ass — can be seen everywhere, as there is a palpable air of positive thinking among Americans. For example, a cab driver in Los Angeles was absolutely serious (if, perhaps, a bit delusional) when he told me that it was only bad luck that had prevented him from being offered (as he put it) the job of President of the country.

In the UK, one is less likely to see such unbridled confidence and enthusiasm. Someone who presents an opportunity to a colleague is more likely to be met with pessimism and caution. We tend to see the glass as half-empty rather than half-full. I find this very disappointing and would urge you to develop a positive attitude toward what you do. The skill and commitment may be there in abundance, but a negative or cautious approach can undermine your potential every time.

Adversity

Looking back over my career, one thing is absolutely certain: the only times when I learned critically important lessons about the difficulties and complexities of business — and about my own capabilities and "bottle" — were during periods of adversity. When times are good, one seldom learns much that is useful, but when times turn bad we find out what we're made of and rise to the occasion.

Though very few would actually welcome adversity, my advice is to see it for what it is and make the most of it: learn how to face it, learn how to cope with it, keep your feet on the ground, and when it has passed look back to see what you could have learned from it.

I knew a young manager in a very large company who was doing extremely well and receiving excellent appraisals — indeed, at one time he was the youngest manager in the organisation. Unexpectedly, he had a change of boss and the new one had a very different opinion of his performance. The new boss — who was called "Smiling Death" behind his back — was very hard on the young manager and told him that he did not measure up to the standards he was expecting. The young manager had never experienced anything like it before and it nearly broke him. But to his credit, he hung in there and eventually became a very effective manager.

Today, that not-so-young manager says that he owes his success to the tough times he had under "Smiling Death". He now feels that he indeed was not up to scratch at the time and that his previous boss was too soft and praised him too easily. He learned from adversity, and it made him a much better manager.

Dealing with stress is obviously an important aspect of adversity. Stress is part and parcel of our working lives and we all need to know how to cope with it when it strikes.

I had a client with a major finance organisation who had been told by the CEO that he could opt for early retirement if he wished. My client was delighted by this news and started to make preparations. But when he mentioned this to his own boss he was told quite clearly that early retirement was not an option. My client referred to his discussion with the CEO who, unfortunately, denied that any such offer had been made. My client, who was 55 at the time and a hard-working, conscientious and loyal manager, was devastated by this turn of events and became highly stressed. His work then suffered and eventually his boss arranged for him to come to me for some advice. We discussed the matter and I was able to convince him not to let his excellent work over the years be swept away by this "misunderstanding". We agreed on a detailed action plan to deal with the problem. Eventually, he was able to put aside his negative approach for a far more positive one and went on to do excellent work for the company. The point here is that stressful situations will occur, but that they don't need to destroy your life if you take appropriate positive measures to deal with them.

Perception

In recent years, it seems that perception — how one is perceived by others — has become critically important to success for managers. There was a time when annual appraisals were crucial, as good ones often meant that a promotion would follow. I would argue that today, though, what is said about you in the corridors of power is even more important than the actual results you've achieved. Clearly, results are still important, but they are almost just what is expected of you, and actual advancement is more likely to be based on how you are perceived.

Perception, therefore, is important and needs to be worked on. You need to understand how others see you. As a start, you might ask during assessment or appraisal meetings with your boss or colleagues to have the papers put aside for a moment and get an honest, off-the-record assessment of how you are perceived generally. You must be careful not to get defensive or to explain yourself if the perceptions are negative. Just listen carefully, take notes and thank them for their honest evaluation. Remember, to a certain extent perception *is* reality so that even if you feel that the criticism is unfair, you need to understand how to change the *perception* others have of you.

For example, you might hear comments like "Do you know that in meetings you give the impression that you are only interested in what *you* are saying?" or ". . . that you always have to have the last say . . ." or ". . . that you never listen . . ." or ". . . that you say very little, sit on the fence and appear to be indecisive . . ." or ". . . that you are too nice and are afraid to make tough decisions . . ." If you become aware that you are viewed in certain ways you can then resolve to do something about it. If you are not aware of how you are perceived, you are likely to continue acting the same way.

To repeat: how you are perceived is of critical importance and it is up to you to manage it if you want to advance in the organisation. You need to have the "bottle" to face up to these perceptions and take action to change them. Talk to your boss, talk to your colleagues, talk to your partner or family, but resolve to make improvements where necessary.

And remember that perceptions *can* change. I had a client who received a very positive annual appraisal except that he was told that he was not "steely" enough. He returned to his office and told his deputy of the criticism and she nearly fell off her seat. She said that his team of 160 people had great respect for his "steeliness" and firmness and actually felt that he could ease up somewhat in that regard. My client decided that he wasn't going to change in any way but told his deputy that it would be useful to spread the word about how the division was really run. At his next appraisal, he again received praise for his performance and was complimented on how much he had improved his "steeliness". He was warned, however, not to go over the top and become too tough!

The point of the above story is that it is simply not enough just to perform well — you also need to be *seen* to be performing well and that is something that needs attention and care.

As you may have noticed, the notion of integrity has already cropped up a couple of times and will do so throughout the book; in fact, Chapter 7 is devoted to it. It was underscored as an important aspect of "bottle" and in general is key to managing yourself. Despite the danger of repetition, no apology will be made for this emphasis. The intention is simply to make the point that integrity is a key component of becoming a whole manager — and that none of us can be reminded too often of the importance of integrity in our lives.

Finally, let me reiterate the importance of always working at managing yourself. You need to appraise on a regular basis what is going well and what you find difficult. Take time to brainstorm how you can build on the former and what specific actions you can take to tackle the latter. The following chapter on Managing Your Time should be of help in this regard. And re-member: if you can't manage yourself effectively, it is very unlikely you will be able to manage anyone else!

Chapter Two

MANAGING YOUR TIME

Time — Your Most Precious Possession

The world is estimated to be around 5 billion years old and one hopes that it will last at least the same again. Thus, although we may feel that time passes far too quickly when things are going well — and too slowly when they are not — in reality our overall time on the planet is relatively minuscule. Yet most people fail to give time the respect it deserves. Make no mistake about it: time is a key, unalterable fact of life — it is your nugget of gold, something to be treasured, appreciated, respected and used very carefully.

This chapter discusses the critical importance of time management and explains why an appreciation of time is fundamental to achieving success without sacrificing your soul. It contains suggestions on how to make the most of your time, how to avoid being a slave to it, and how to make it work for you rather than against you. It also includes some practical suggestions on how to develop time management techniques that will help you stay on top of this essential resource.

Dealing with Time

Most managers would agree that "finding the time" is one of the key difficulties they face in achieving success and fulfilment at work and at home. Time to manage their departments effectively, time to develop new skills, time to make long-term decisions, time to provide support for their staff, time to read new reports and books, time to take physical exercise, time to spend with their families, etc., etc., etc. For many managers, the pressures of time can often seem overwhelming.

It is critical, therefore, that you devise a strategy for dealing with time. The first step is to commit to a specific plan for how you allot your time. This can cover a host of areas — short term or long term, personal or business. Although the above may seem obvious, it is still worth stating — without a conscious plan people tend to be reactive, behaving like a fish without a tail. Without a plan you will be much less effective than you should be, and are likely to become frustrated and unfulfilled. You are also like to *appear* as if you are not in complete control and, as we will see throughout this book, how you are perceived by others is of critical importance.

Naturally, events will occur that are unplanned, and I am not arguing here that every moment needs to be rigidly laid out. However, if you generally plan well, unexpected events can be dealt with smoothly and with a minimum of disruption. Above all, being in control of your time will lead to increased self-confidence and peace of mind — and, best of all, with a bit of self-discipline and thought it can be achieved by anyone.

Developing a New Mindset

A key aspect to the successful management of time lies in developing a mindset so strong that it guides everything you do. I have a client in marketing who says that she approaches time in the same way she approaches her customers. In fact, she looks at time as a customer — and not just an ordinary one but the most important customer she will ever have. Consider the wisdom of this approach. When treating customers that are vital to our interests (whether internal or external customers) we are careful never to take anything for granted; we would never treat them lightly and would always give them our best. We need to look at time in the same way.

Another client of mine thinks of himself as his managing director of time and his imaginary board as being made up of four directors: long-term business; short-term business; long-term personal; and short-term personal. These four directors are answerable for how their time is used and then must negotiate with the others to argue their case! Clearly, this client has an active imagination, but whatever method is used the key is to look at time as the most important resource at your control and to act accordingly.

Managing Your Diary

How you use your diary is clearly a key element in effective time management. If properly used, your diary can keep you organised and focused on the key events well in advance. Everyone will have their own preference on the type of diary used, but whatever format it takes, you should keep it simple and flexible. Above all, it should be one that you are comfortable with. The following is based on paper-based diaries but the same concepts will apply to electronic versions.

The Diary Layout

After studying a wide range of diary systems and formats, I decided to produce my own to fit my particular needs. Many of my clients now use it as well, and anyone is free to adopt or modify it as needed.

In a four-ring A4 binder I have a full-month calendar on the left-hand side and a detailed day-by-day diary on the right. In this way, I can see at a glance what my commitments are for the month, as well as viewing the specific meetings and activities planned for the day. In my mind, this is an ideal way to be organised for both the short and long term, and even has advantages over electronic diaries, which can be slow and cumbersome to use.

The two-page layout is illustrated on pages 20–21, though obviously it has been reduced considerably to fit a book page.

As you can see, it is easy to enter times of meetings and other business activities. I always try to avoid back-to-back meetings so that I can take time for telephone calls and other matters, as well as to take notes on the previous meeting and prepare for the next. I also enter a dot where meetings are held in my office and a dot with a circle around it for meetings or activities outside the office. You will, of course, devise your own methods, but I find it useful to know at a glance when I will be out of the office.

Clients often question me on how to schedule their time when so much of their work is reactionary — "putting out fires" and the like. If you have that kind of job, my advice is to understand when you are least likely to be interrupted — say, early in the morning or late in the day — and avoid arranging appointments at those times so that you can focus on other tasks. Of course, there are times when you will need to be flexible and schedule meetings at short notice, but in general I would urge you to resist the temptation to be constantly changing dates for meetings and try to stick whenever possible to the original schedule.

By adopting this simple monthly and daily calendar system, you will quickly become organised and time-efficient. Your diary is your most valuable tool, so if you are not treating yours with the respect it deserves, I suggest you start doing so today.

Monthly Calendar

	8	9	10	11	12	1	2	3	4	5	6	Evening
Fri 1												
Sat 2												
Sun 3												
Mon 4												
Tues 5												
Wed 6												
Thur 7												
Fri 8												
Sat 9												
Sun 10												
Mon 11												
Tues 12												
Wed 13												
Thur 14												
Fri 15												
Sat 16												
Sun 17												
Mon 18												
Tues 19												
Wed 20												
Thur 21												
Fri 22												
Sat 23												
Sun 24												
Mon 25												
Tues 26												
Wed 27												
Thur 28												
Fri 29												
Sat 30												
Sun 31												

Daily Calendar

Day: Date:

Appointments	Top 6
8.00	
9.00	
10.00	
11.00	Other Action Points
12.00	
1.00	
2.00	
3.00	Telephone
4.00	
5.00	
6.00	
Notes	

Punctuality

A key component of time management — and one often ignored — is the whole area of punctuality. The importance of punctuality extends beyond time management, of course, as it involves common courtesy as well, but I find that people who are unable to manage their time invariably lack punctuality as well.

In a nutshell: never be late for a meeting — *never*! One reason is that you in effect incur penalty points for being late and thus could be giving away an advantage. Another reason, though, is that there is a snowball effect to being late, as subsequent meetings or activities are pushed back, which obviously will lead to time management problems.

How can you ensure you are never late? Well, it is possible. For example, you could automatically add extra time to all journeys — ten minutes, half an hour, an hour, whatever — to take account of likely motorway hold-ups, train delays or other typical excuses for being late. If you are early for a meeting you can always use the time to catch up on business reading, preparation for other meetings, pending file and so on. Remember to always carry such material in your briefcase and count it as a blessing if you can find a half hour somewhere to catch up on paperwork.

Become a person with a reputation for always being on time and it will pay back healthy dividends. You will also be more relaxed and better focused, and will be able to approach business matters with more confidence. Furthermore, you should treat your personal appointments in exactly the same way. Be on time for dinners with your partner, birthday parties for your children and all other personal events. It will show that you value the occasion and those associated with it, and that you are not making the unforgivable, but all too frequent, mistake of putting your work life ahead of your home life.

Practical Time Management Strategies

In deciding to tackle time management problems in a serious way, one thing is certain: some kind of system is vital. It is not enough just to be determined that you will manage your time more efficiently from now on. You need to find or develop a system that will enable you — or force you! — to be very disciplined about time. There are numerous commercial systems and strategies available, but in my mind most are unnecessarily complicated and overly intricate. Instead, I would recommend an approach that has worked extremely well with my clients: the Four Point Time Driver.

Four Point Time Driver

Here are the four elements of the Four Point Time Driver approach:

1. Six top priorities are identified and completed daily.

2.   Three-hour sessions for quality thinking are scheduled for every two weeks.

3.   Your diary is checked every other day for activities six to eight weeks ahead.

4.   Make active use of a "bring forward files" system.

Like most good time management systems, you will find this approach to be simple and straight-forward enough. It is also, however, highly effective. Here is the thinking behind each point.

Six Top Priorities

This point obviously will force you to think through each day what actions need to be completed as a matter of urgency. There is nothing magical about the number six, but in my experience trying to do more than that will lead to frustration and inefficiency — in other words, where you were before you adopted this approach!

The top six priorities will consist of the things that have to be done that day at all costs, including tasks that you would otherwise want to avoid. And please note that the top six priorities may include items in your personal life as well as business tasks. A typical top six list may look like this:

1.   Debrief boss following key meeting.

2.   Prepare for team development planning meeting.

3. Book restaurant for wedding anniversary.

4. Complete first draft of report for major meeting scheduled five weeks ahead.

5. Deal with pending file — 25 per cent minimum.

6. Arrange department away-day think tank.

Now all you have to do is to ensure that these six points are completed by the end of the day. Sounds easy enough, but to start with you will do well to complete three or four. However, if you persevere you will eventually develop the habit of completing all six. You can compile these lists at the beginning of the work day, or at the end of the previous day, or even as you are going to work. The important thing is that you always list the points that matter, and that you are diligent in completing the tasks that you have identified.

Three Hour Quality Thinking Sessions

This point will be one that very few currently practise — much to their detriment. Indeed, managers who feel that they are slaves to time seldom feel that they can devote specific periods to "quality thinking". If they did, however, they would be amazed at how much more effective — and time efficient — they had become.

These sessions are your own private individual think tanks. They are designed for thinking through the really big issues, the major questions that will ultimately determine the success of you and your team. They might involve long-term strategic issues, major new initiatives, radical new departures, whatever. But these are the issues where you truly add value to your job — without this thinking, you are just doing the bare essentials and not meeting your potential.

To be effective, these sessions must be scheduled and taken seriously. Preferably, they would be conducted in some neutral place where there would be no distractions, such as a hotel sitting area or library or somewhere else you can sit without being disturbed such as on a train or a plane. It is usually not possible to do it at home and it definitely cannot be done at the office.

As with any other meetings, you should be sure you are well prepared. Keep the papers you take with you to a minimum, as they can clutter your thinking, and don't attempt to cover too many topics. Typically, two or three issues, and never more than four, are the right number to consider in any one session. The only discipline you need to impose on yourself is that, following these think-tank sessions, you write up an action plan outlining the necessary steps you need to take, research to be done, people to meet with, and so on. You then transfer these details to your diary and stick to them. Failure to do so renders the whole exercise useless.

In addition to the obvious benefits of taking time to think through serious issues, the *process* of quality thinking time is very beneficial. Your brain, both the conscious and subconscious parts, will be fully engaged on the issues at hand, which should result in much clearer and higher-quality thinking. In addition, your self-confidence will get a boost, as you know that you are giving adequate time to considering the big issues, rather than having them sneak up on you when you are snowed under with the daily requirements of your job.

Do not underestimate the importance of this activity. Most of my clients claim that this regular three-hour quality thinking session is the best single piece of advice they have ever received. Start today.

Diary Check Every Other Day

This is a very simple activity that will help you to stay on top of your schedule. By being aware at all times of activities six to eight weeks ahead, you will ensure that you have adequate time to think through and prepare for whatever is required. Again, you will be in control of time rather than being its slave.

Every other day you should carefully check your diary six to eight weeks ahead and note any actions that need to be taken. Repeating this activity so often eliminates any possibility of being caught unawares by some major event suddenly sneaking up on you. Also, your subconscious again will be working away in the background while you are focusing on the key priorities of the day. And don't underestimate the power of the subconscious!

Bring Forward Files

Here is another extremely useful tool for dealing with work overload, in this case excessive paperwork. It will allow you to clear your desk and briefcase of the piles of memos, letters, etc. that gather there, and also help to give you a reputation for being organised and having a memory like an elephant.

Basically, the "bring forward file" is just a concertina file with 31 pockets for each day of the month. Every piece of paper that you do not have to deal with straight away you place into the pocket appropriate to the time you wish to deal with it. For example, if you have a memo you do not have to consider for a week, you place it in the appropriate pocket, and similarly for ones to deal with at the end of the month.

Another example would be if someone informed you they would get you some information by a certain date, then you would make a note of the fact and place it in the appropriate pocket. When the date arrives you would take it out and, if you still do not have the information, you could then call to enquire on its status. Before long, you would have a reputation as someone who expects things to happen on the dates promised, as well as being efficient in following up on projects. Letters, memos, reminders, press articles, etc., can all be handled in this way. If you have a secretary or assistant, you can just put B/F (bring forward) with an appropriate date on each.

This is a very simple system, but you will be impressed at how it helps you to clear your desk and attend to matters when they require it. Again, you will be putting yourself in charge of managing your time.

Other Methods for Saving Time

Here are some additional suggestions for simple changes you can make to free up some time:

- Before all meetings, whether one-to-one or in a group, decide on a start time and a finish time and keep to both.

- Stand up while making a phone call – for some reason this helps to keep them short and to the point.

- When the paperwork is unusually heavy, take time to sort it out into four piles in order of importance:

  ◊ Urgent/important

  ◊ Urgent/general

  ◊ Not urgent/important

  ◊ Not urgent/general.

- Use the quiet time around Christmas to carry out major administrative work.

- Go through one file a week and throw out any papers not needed.

- Pretend each Friday that you are about to go on holiday for three weeks . . .

- Remember that you have two ears and one mouth and they should be used accordingly.

- Organise your weekend diary as effectively as your business one.

- Don't forget to take a break to recharge your batteries a couple of times a day — you'll return much refreshed and more efficient.

Time is a Journey

So often people get angry — mostly with themselves — because they've missed an opportunity or something has gone wrong in their life. But the real test of time is how such situations are treated, how people recover and get back on track. Time can be a great motivator, and will be forgiving if treated with respect and not taken for granted. There is often time to change, to have another go, to correct, to learn, to do better.

All journeys have a flow and an end, and the question you should ask yourself is "what have you done with the time you have been given?" A good answer would be that you always had a plan and made the most of each day, week, month and year work-wise, partnership-wise, family-wise, personally-wise and so on. I found the job I really wanted to do when I was 53 and started my consultancy. Perhaps I was a late developer, and maybe you are as well, but the point is that time is the most precious possession you have, your nugget of gold, and I urge you to treasure it accordingly.

Chapter Three

GETTING THINGS DONE

When all is said and done, to achieve success — however you define it — you will need to gain a reputation throughout your career for getting things done. That means that you will first need to prioritise the key activities that are important in your department, company or division, and then you will have to devise techniques or methods to ensure that they actually happen. These are fundamentals in any position of authority and this chapter will offer some helpful tips on how to be sure that you are a manager who gets things done.

In this chapter, we will first look at two simple techniques you can use to help you to get things done, and at how focusing on your top six priorities can be useful in this regard. We will conclude with a discussion of the importance of managing with vision.

What follows will focus on the workplace, but it is important to note that these techniques can also apply in the home. As discussed elsewhere in this book, one of the keys to becoming a whole manager is to find the right balance between the workplace and the home, and this includes such issues as prioritising, decision-making, etc. — in other words, getting things done.

Ongoing Tasks and One-off Projects

Most managers will have responsibility for two different kinds of activities: those that are ongoing, day-to-day ones and those that are special one-off projects. For the former, there is a very simple technique to ensure that the important daily activities are dealt with, as well as ensuring that those above and below you in the organisation are aware of, and in agreement with, the need for those activities — it's called the Two Pager. This technique, which is described below, will allow you to manage the workflow in a sensible and relaxed way — even in times of stress and work overload.

For one-off projects, the management task is very different, as you will have to decide what needs to be done, how it should be done, who will be doing it, and so on. Again, however, there are relatively simple tools that can help you to organise yourself and your staff to accomplish what needs to be done. One is called the Triangle Approach — though, as you will see, it develops into a pentagon!

The Two Pager

I once had a client from a large company who felt that he was doing very good work but that it was not being appreciated by his boss. Similarly, he felt that he was so engrossed in his own pressures that he was not taking notice of the input being made by his own managers. This is a fairly common situation facing people in all types of organisations — and a fairly dangerous one. Not only is the lack of communication a major concern, but the lack of appreciation and feedback will inevitably adversely affect job performance.

My client and I decided that lack of communication was the prime cause of his problems and devised a solution that would not only help him to communicate the activities of his department upwards to his boss, but also downwards to his staff and sideways to other departments. Basically, we came up with a concise document that would describe the department's activities on an ongoing basis and that would be presented to my client's boss for his input and, ultimately, his approval. This would accomplish two things: first, it would allow the boss to feel that he was directly involved with the activities of the department — without requiring a huge amount of his time — and it would make him more aware, and it was hoped more appreciative, of the activities of the department and my client's role in managing them.

The Two Pager Format

The Two Pager is designed to provide a snapshot of the department. The first section begins with a description of the main responsibilities, structure, personnel and relationships of the department, as well as how it fits into the organisation as a whole. Any key issues should be highlighted as well as any other relevant information as appropriate. Due to the constant change organisations are facing today, any relevant developments, data or trends should be noted. Anyone new to the organisation should be able to get a clear grasp of this department from the description in the opening section.

The next section would describe the key objectives of the department, most of which should be quantifiable and thus able to be measured. Many of these objectives would be linked to financial and volume matters — profit, targets, etc. — but some could also relate to personnel issues and other more subjective matters.

The final section would consist of ten or so key ongoing tasks which need to be carried out to ensure that the prime objectives are achieved. A sample Two Pager for the sales department in a fictional company is shown on pages 38–39, but obviously the objectives and key tasks could be very different for other kinds of organisations.

To return to my client: he submitted his draft Two Pager, which was greeted with enthusiasm by his boss who agreed to use it to appraise my client's progress every four months. It became the basis for salary reviews and his boss was so impressed by the idea that he produced his own Two Pager so that his boss — a board director — could manage his activities better! My client then used the Two Pager approach with the team of managers reporting to him and they in turn used it to manage those down the line — from such little acorns do oak trees grow . . .

The Two Pager has considerable potential, but one point is vital: never let it gather dust on the top of a shelf. Be sure that it is discussed and updated at least three times a year and that it becomes a prime checklist and appraisal/measurement document. Properly used, it can be a strong motivational tool and can help ensure that things get done.

The Triangle Approach

While the Two Pager is ideal for ongoing responsibilities, a different approach is needed for major, one-off projects. In this case, you will need something that can cover all the key issues and aspects yet at the same time remain simple and straightforward. Indeed, in terms of getting things done, it is almost always advisable to keep your approach focused and uncomplicated. A device that can be extremely useful in this regard in terms of planning large projects was developed by Marketing Solutions in London in the mid-1980s. We called it the Triangle Approach for reasons that will be made apparent by the diagram shown on page 40.

Sample Two Pager for Company X

The Marketplace

The price war in the retail market over the last 18 months has resulted in a reduction in operators, and a serious fall off in profitability to both company suppliers and owners. Those who remain are under pressure firstly to operate more efficiently and identify other profit opportunities, and also to offer a much improved level of customer service.

Whereas Company Y (market share approximately 23%) has been leading the retail marketing thrust, their lack of funding is now working against them. Company Z (16%), the other main competitor, having recently acquired Company A, is flexing its marketing muscle and becoming increasingly active in new product development.

The Opportunity

The opportunity for Company X is to continue to build strong relationships with operators to establish single image consistency across the network and to capitalise on the excellence package which ensures the shop is a serious profit centre. In conclusion, the main task facing the Consumer Sales team is to ensure that Company X representation in areas where there are no company sites is of the highest standard, so that the outlets make a serious contribution to both market share and profit.

Key Tasks

1. Ensure each team member understands the part they play in how to achieve the consumer sales objectives and have an implementation plan which is regularly reviewed and followed up.

2. Ensure that the coaching carried out for members of the team is focused on accompaniments and training sessions which are linked to the quarterly appraisals.

3. Develop a system whereby the technical and personal competencies of each member is appraised quarterly and appropriate developmental action is taken.

4. Ensure that there are specific arrangements in place which lead to the achievement of the agreed network plan. Make input into the future network planning re feasibility.

5. Take steps to learn from Europe and where suitable apply these in the UK – all part of Company X's best practice philosophy.

6. Take steps to ensure that Company X's company standards for safety, driving and health are understood and practised by all personnel within consumer sales.

7. Develop an approach to engender a high level of enthusiasm, commitment and individual fulfilment as part of the new Company X culture.

1. Where To?
Decide objectives/goals and
place in order of priority.

2. How To?
Produce
planning paper
geared to
ensuring that
each objective/
goal is achieved.

3. Who Does What?
Decide on the best
organisation
procedures and
personnel to
achieve objectives.

Step 1: Where To?

The first step is to discuss, consider, brainstorm, etc. about what you are trying to accomplish. You need to consider very carefully the direction of the project, taking note of the barriers that may get in your way, until you are sure you've got it right. You then need to decide on the objectives or goals and place them in order of importance. Focus on the key ones and omit any that are irrelevant or unimportant.

Step 2: How To?

You will need to adopt a very firm approach here: what specific plans or tasks will be needed to achieve each objective or goal? You need to be sure to avoid grey areas or foggy thinking — high quality, concise thinking is essential. Again, you should omit any tasks that are not linked to specific goals or objectives.

Step 3: Who Does What?

Now comes the crunch: what kind of people, and in what kind of structure or organisation, will be needed to ensure the success of the plan? You should begin by ignoring the structure of the current organisation so that your thinking is uncluttered and not hampered by the status quo. You then need to write down precisely what skills and characteristics will be required for this project. If you have concerns that some team members will not meet your requirements, you might consider breaking the groups down into small teams of three or four so that weaker members will be supported by stronger ones. And obviously if you feel that the initiative may fail because you don't have the right people available, you will need to discuss the implications of that with your boss or human resources director.

During Step 3 you will also need to determine what procedures or IT systems will be needed to implement the plans successfully. You will need to avoid falling into the trap of allowing IT systems and procedures to become separate entities with their own agendas, however. They should just be viewed as an effective means of facilitating the needs of the project.

Those are the three crucial sides of the triangle that need to be carefully addressed before the project can get off the ground. I would suggest, however, that to be truly successful we will need to add two more sides and in effect turn the triangle into a pentagon.

1. Where To?
Decide objectives/goals and
place in order of priority.

2. How To?
Produce planning
paper geared to
ensuring that
each objective/
goal is achieved.

3. Who Does What?
Decide on the best
organisation procedures
and personnel to achieve
objectives.

4. Monitor
Continually
check on
progress of all
tasks

5. Review
Look again at
first four steps
to be sure they
are appropriate.

Step 4: Monitor

Always monitor your progress. Be sure that you have clear milestones for each important activity in your diary. One company I know established a critical path for major projects whereby vital milestones were represented by little pictures of champagne bottles — and at the completion of the project, actual bottles were purchased to celebrate successful completion of the project! Another company built a three-dimensional mock-up of a critical path out of PVC boarding with suitable models visualising the key milestones and left it in a common area. The key point is to monitor the progress of the project in a way that everyone can see and appreciate.

Step 5: Review

It is critical to have regular review meetings, whereby you determine where you are doing well, where you are behind, and where you might need help. You need to revisit steps 1–4 to check that each is still appropriate and to decide on any follow-up action.

That is the basic Pentagon Approach to managing key projects. It is simple, straightforward and effective, and I recommend that you put it into use and adapt it as needed for your own initiatives. Incidentally, this approach is not restricted solely to the workplace. It can also be useful for holiday planning, career planning, weddings, or for any other kind of project that needs to be broken down into discrete activities, and then monitored carefully.

Back to the Top Six Priorities

As discussed in the previous chapter, focusing on six top priorities can be a useful way to avert time management problems, but it can also be extremely useful in terms of being a manager who gets things done. In other words, they are not just a short-term solution but also a key tool in achieving long-term goals. For example, assume that you are working on a major initiative which involves a progress meeting with the key players in six weeks' time. Your short-term task might be to write the first draft of the key issues for the meeting — attendees, research, charts, etc. — but you would also need to plan your diary appointments six to eight weeks ahead for the key meetings, events or activities for which you need to be prepared. Thus the short-term action is linked to longer-term quality — which helps to ensure that you will get the results you want.

As noted in the previous chapter, it is important to focus in a concentrated way on no more than six points on a daily basis. Any more than that and I believe quality will suffer considerably. Indeed, for those issues that fall outside the top six, you may have to accept that a good deal less than 100 per cent is all you can afford to give to those tasks. You simply do not need to go all out on every issue — and trying to do so can be a recipe for disaster. So give your maximum attention to your top six and I guarantee you will not regret it.

Let's now look at what the top six points might be for a typical manager. This should help to illustrate how this approach might work in practise.

First, the manager needs to focus on the Two Pager — the manager's bible for ensuring that the top priorities are being met and that they are communicated upwards, downwards and laterally in the organisation. This might include the following actions in the six points on different days:

1. Book date in diary to discuss with managers achievements of key tasks.

2. Use meeting to update page one background and highlight new key issues. Ensure that major actions

needed to ensure that objectives are met are being carried out.

3. Book date with boss to discuss updated Two Pager and to identify key issues that require discussion or answers.

4. Ensure Two Pager is used as checklist every two weeks.

5. Enter updated Two Pager for inclusion in upcoming think tank session.

The Two Pager is nearly always included as one of the top six priorities.

The second point might be to clear at least half of your "pending" tray. This could entail selecting all items that need action immediately or within the next two weeks and dealing with them accordingly. Non-essential items can be left pending, but you will be aware that you are on top of the issues that need immediate attention.

The third point could be to make a decision about your holidays for the year. As frequently mentioned in this book, to be a successful manager you need to find the right balance between your work life and home life. In this case, you might select two ideal dates to take your holidays, discuss with your partner and family what they would like to do, and then decide to take one break during the Easter holidays and another for your summer vacation. Your family will be grateful that, despite the pressures you are under, you have taken the time to plan your holidays.

The fourth point might be to prepare the first draft of a speech that your boss has asked you to make to your American partners in three months at the head office. You would need to do the necessary research and data-gathering for the speech, and since this is a longer-term project, different aspects of it might be one of your top six action points for the next few months.

Point number five could conceivably be to discuss with your deputy an unfortunate habit he has developed of giving the impression that he is always right — no matter who he is talking to. This is the kind of thing that can be continually put off, but in this case you decide to meet with him at 6.00 to discuss it so that he can dwell on it overnight.

Finally, point number six could be some special new project that you need to initiate. Unlike the Two Pager, this would be a one-off project that requires a different approach — like the Triangle Approach discussed above.

Managing with Vision

Finally, all successful managers should be able to see the big picture in any situation — not just long-term issues such as what the marketing plan might look like in five years, but larger strategic issues that lie at the heart of the organisation. Often, being aware of the big picture and what is really important will lead to an automatic understanding of how to be a manager who gets things done.

You need to ask yourself questions like, "What impact could this issue have on our positioning in three years?" or "What happens if we get this decision wrong — who is affected and how?" or "What is the long-term impact if we take a short-term view on this matter today?" The answers to such questions can be somewhat intangible — which is why they often are not asked — but a good manager will have the big picture in mind at all times. And, if you can manage with vision you may earn a well-deserved reputation as someone who gets things done.

Chapter Four

MANAGING YOUR TEAM

In order to be a successful manager it is clear that you need to get high quality work out of the people who report to you. No matter how capable you are personally, you will not be able to accomplish much all on your own. You will need a well-motivated, efficient and enthusiastic team working with you.

As noted earlier, managers today feel that there are numerous barriers preventing them from becoming effective all-round managers. Pressures from shareholders, senior executives and others mean that increased productivity is essential, and the only way to achieve that is through skilful management of their teams.

This chapter addresses all the key elements of managing downwards, including advice on how to be inspirational instead of just motivational, how to stimulate individuals to grow, how to perform simple and clear appraisals, how to make meetings work, and how to get the right balance between criticism and praise. In addition, the chapter will focus on how to maximise the effectiveness of training and development, as well as covering the "steel" factor and the "fun" factor, both of which are essential elements of managing.

The Key Resource

Managers are increasingly aware that competitive advantage stems not from products, systems or processes — but from people. In fact, there are only two resources in any organisation. First, there is money, without which nothing happens, and second is people, which ultimately will determine the organisation's success or failure. The real strength of a company, department or unit, however, is greater than the sum of its parts. The extra component comes from the morale, enthusiasm, positive approach and mutual respect found between management and employees.

It is vital that managers be fully aware that their own success depends on their ability to get the best out of their staff. This means not only ensuring that each team member performs their job well, but that they also develop and grow to be able to meet future challenges.

Newly appointed managers need to understand that they have a profound effect on those reporting to them. They are suddenly expected to solve problems, give direction, perform their own jobs while helping others perform theirs, be a mentor, a role model and much more. Often they will miss the camaraderie and friendship they felt as part of the team, but unfortunately it will no longer be possible to be "one of them". It is now more important to be respected than to be popular, and that can often be a lonely experience. But the truth is that as a manager you need to take responsibility for your department or team, which requires a new mindset and different skills.

So how do you meet the challenge of helping staff members to develop while at the same time meeting individual or company goals or targets? Below are some suggestions.

Do Unto Others . . .

One way to start your thinking is simply to consider how you would like to be managed and then try to apply that to how you manage others. One client I had said that he would like to have a boss who "knows where he or she is going, is focused on priorities, is good at handling adversity, gives me space but guides me when things go wrong, lets me know how I'm doing and where I can improve". He then tries to keep this mental image in mind when dealing with his own staff members.

Making People Feel They Matter

To get excellent results, it is no longer enough just to motivate your team. You need to inspire the team as a whole and the individuals within it. You need to convince your team to choose to follow the course you are suggesting — unlike the old days when people were expected to do as they were told. In today's competitive environment you need to get maximum effort and commitment from each team member, and the way to accomplish that is to treat them as valued and essential components of the group.

Many books on motivation stress the importance of giving praise as a positive motivator of people. Praise is clearly an essential part of managing, and when it is given it is crucial that it is not qualified or it will lose its impact. The praise should be heartfelt and direct, along the lines of "Well done, that was a great result!". You should also tell your peers and others in the team so that the positive response can be spread throughout the group.

One of my clients discovered that her team, not surprisingly, tended to be much more highly motivated when she heaped praise on them. The more she praised them the harder they worked and the better their results. Naturally, she used this fact to inspire her team. For example, when she saw that people were easing up she would withhold her positive remarks because she found that in order to gain favour her team would step up their endeavours. This approach worked for her.

There is also, however, a strong case to be made for the benefits of constructive criticism. Whereas few managers have any difficulty with giving praise, many do have a problem with delivering criticism. No one likes to dwell on the negative, especially with employees who do not take criticism well, but it is an essential part of the manager's job to help employees improve their performance. There are many ways to give constructive criticism, but the best is using an interrogative approach whereby the manager asks questions that help the employees themselves identify the areas of weakness and the need for improvement. The tone should be constructive and positive, yet firm and unambiguous. The employees should come away with a clear understanding of the nature of the problem and the expected response.

Using both praise and constructive criticism will let people know that they matter and that their contributions to the group are valued. It is a key component to developing a strong spirit in the organisation.

Build on Strengths

One company I did some work with placed a great deal of importance on training courses, and in particular on employees achieving high marks on them. For example, everyone in the sales department was expected to take courses on interpersonal skills, negotiation, administration, and so on. Someone who received low marks on a course had to repeat it until the requisite score was achieved. In other words, a salesperson who was very strong on interpersonal skills, but weak on administration, would need to spend hours working on the latter — much to the detriment of the former. The obvious result was a much less effective employee.

The clear lesson of the above is that managers should first of all look for strengths and then build on them. This will lead to a sense of self-confidence and well-being that is much more likely to lead to success than focusing overmuch on supposed weaknesses. In fact, organisations that focus on their employees' strengths find that the weaknesses gradually disappear as well, probably because the feeling of self-confidence allows the employee to tackle more effectively and improve on those areas where they need work.

This obviously does not mean ignoring weaknesses that are important to performance. These need to be discussed fully and addressed through training, work experience, setting of objectives, and so on. But the goal for a manager is to get the best from their employees, not that they necessarily excel in all things, and the way to do that is to build on their natural strengths so that their confidence is high.

Performance Appraisals

There are a great many lengthy and detailed appraisal forms available these days, often produced by highly reputable and professional experts. One company I work with includes analysis on 32 separate competencies for its employees. I question, however, whether the time and effort expended on such detailed staff appraisals are truly necessary. As with many other things, I would argue that a focus on simplicity, clarity and conciseness will get far better results.

Working with one of my clients, we developed the following format which I would suggest could be a model for others:

Questions	Points out of 10
1. Is the person prioritised?	[ ]
2. Does the person make the right things happen very well?	[ ]
3. Does the person inspire others to make the right things happen very well?	[ ]
4. Is the person strong on attention to detail and following up?	[ ]

Where the marks are high, say 8 to 10, ask yourself why, and there you have the strengths. Where the marks are low, say 0 to 5, again ask yourself why, and there you have the weaknesses. The advantage of this simple scheme is that it relies on your perceptions and impressions of the employee's work — and is thus quite correctly subjective — rather than being based on a complicated set of responses, which might be objectively "correct" but not necessarily give a true view of the person's performance.

After completing the above exercise for each member of your team you should be able to identify the strengths and weaknesses of each. For example, point number three, dealing with the employee's ability to inspire others, will be an indicator of that person's management potential. You can then prepare a development programme for each person including basic needs, specific training, work experience requirements and so on as required for that individual. This analysis should be carried out regularly, at least every six months, in order to chart that person's progress in the organisation.

Training

For some reason, employee training is seen in many organisations as the responsibility of a separate department, rather than as an integral part of the line manager's job. In reality, it should be the manager's responsibility to determine the individual training needs of their team members and to ensure that they are met. The Training Department can be extremely useful in determining what courses are most suitable as well as organising the courses and suggesting other ideas about how the skills can be developed. The line manager should be sure to follow up on the training to ensure that it was effective and that the new skills or knowledge are being used. For example, prior to the course you might agree with the individual to identify and focus on three of your key points and then have regular meetings afterwards to review progress on them. But again, this is your responsibility, not the training manager's.

The Manager as Coach

All managers are coaches and as organisational structures become flatter this skill will grow in importance. As with coaches in professional sports, the goal of the coach in business is to help the individual to develop to the best of their ability. This involves careful planning and preparation, as well as considerable patience. Regular review sessions are crucial, each ending with an action plan and a date for the next review.

There are a couple of different approaches one can take when acting as a coach. The first is the Questioning Approach, which might include the following:

- "What did you think went well and what was tricky?"

- "If you were to do it again what would you do differently?"

- "How did you go about preparing for the meeting?"

The responses to these kinds of questions give the individual the opportunity to identify for themselves the areas they need to improve. This is obviously more effective than just telling the person what they are doing wrong. This approach encourages ownership by the individual for their development and, once that is established, a positive, jointly agreed action plan can be discussed and devised together.

A second approach could be called the Impression Approach. This might include comments like

- "My feeling is that you can do better than that. Let's talk through your approach."

- "You appear to have had an off day. What changes would you make in the future?"

Here you would be leading the discussion a bit more but still encouraging the individual to identify for themselves specific areas for improvement.

Whatever approach is taken, it is crucial for the manager to ensure that there is an action plan to implement changes and subsequent follow-up. Remember that without follow-up, nearly all coaching and development plans are bound to fail.

"Steeliness"

The need for a manager to gain respect rather than popularity has already been noted. This may involve things like being firm but fair, not capitulating on certain issues, being willing to take responsibility when things go wrong, etc. — all of which I would call "steeliness".

A client of mine in the computer business decided that he needed to develop a suitable replacement for himself as part of his succession planning. He selected a very capable all-round manager whose only weakness was that he was too soft and easy-going. My client decided to coach him on his steeliness, on how to handle adversity, to dig in his heels and stand firm on certain occasions. This became a regular topic at their meetings — which in itself required steeliness from both of them — and eventually a positive change was apparent.

Another client of mine made a very conscious decision to work on his steeliness. He decided every three months to focus on one particular aspect of the business and to be fairly ruthless about it. One period, it might be travel expenses; another, customer complaints, and so on. He was meticulous in studying these specific areas and relentless in his attempts to improve them. This approach had an impact, to say the least, as his team quickly learned that they had to be on their toes at all times. His reputation for steeliness grew as well.

Effective Meetings

In managing your team, you will need to become skilled at two kinds of meetings: one-to-one meetings with individual members and team meetings with the whole group. Both are vital to effective communication and staff development and thus must be made to work. Gaining a reputation for running successful meetings is a worthy goal for any manager, and one that is achievable if you follow some basic rules.

One-to-One Meetings

These are held regularly with people who report to you, either weekly, monthly or whatever is appropriate. Both sides need to prepare in advance and, as with all meetings, there should be an agreed start and finish time which is strictly observed. These meetings are for addressing real issues, not administrative or minor matters that could be dealt with by memo or e-mail. If your team member raises a specific problem, you should listen to their recommendations for a solution and then help them to decide on a correct course of action. Each action point should be noted with a to-do date and the initials of who is responsible. This action plan then becomes the basis of the agenda for the next meeting with other points added as required.

One-to-one meetings should be business-like and efficient, but don't forget to make them human as well. Show an interest in your team member's development, hobbies, opinions, home life and anything else that shows that they matter to you. This is an excellent opportunity to create the kind of spirit and enthusiasm that leads to superior performance.

Many managers succumb to the temptation to cancel or re-schedule these meetings due to other business pressures. Don't do it. This sends a terrible signal to your team member: you're implying that these meetings are not important and, by inference, the team member is not important. This could be seriously de-motivating.

Team Meetings

These meetings are also crucial to good management. Again, preparation is vital for both the manager and team members. Agendas should be distributed several days in advance so that individuals can prepare questions or make presentations as needed.

It is the manager's responsibility to ensure that every team member contributes during the meeting. By asking specific questions or seeking the opinion of quieter members, the manager can make sure that everyone participates. Relatively equal input from all members is crucial to team balance.

At the end of the meeting — no matter what was discussed or what issues arose — everybody should depart feeling inspired and determined to perform to the utmost of their ability. This is the manager's challenge. It is not enough that each member is aware of the action points and the agreed follow-up — they must also come away highly motivated and enthusiastic. Therefore never allow a meeting to end on an inconclusive or discordant note.

Away Days

A very useful way of achieving team commitment and unity is to have regular day-long team meetings outside of the office. These meetings encourage communication across the team and allow team members to make suggestions and ask questions on a wide range of issues. The format for these meetings is important, and below is one that has proved highly successful for several organisations:

- **Beginning Session**: The manager gives an overview of what the team has achieved over the last period. Good and bad overall performance is highlighted, strengths and weaknesses are underlined, other relevant issues of importance are reviewed. It is a time when the manager should communicate overall impressions of what is going well or not well.

- **Middle Session**: The discussion then focuses on what individuals feel could be done to build on the strengths and to remedy any weaknesses. All agreed points are written on flip charts, which are then put in order on the walls around the room. This exercise may take two to four hours, though any longer than that and people are likely to become tired and lose their focus.

- **Final Session**: The final hour is spent pulling together all the points in order of importance and assigning to individuals specific responsibility and dates for completion.

- **In conclusion**: The session ends by agreeing the date for the next away day when progress will be reviewed.

This kind of a meeting can be highly effective in ensuring team involvement and commitment. On the one hand, it allows you as manager to communicate your views and concerns about the performance of your group, thus affirming your leadership. On the other hand, it allows team members to have real input into the process and to agree what actions need to occur, thus affirming their impact and ownership. And, once again, the emphasis on action points and follow-up helps to motivate staff and ensures that changes will be made.

Dealing with Difficult People

Most managers will on occasion have to deal with people they find difficult. The problem might be one of different styles or a personality clash, or it might be that the other person *is* simply difficult to get along with — and it's up to you know which is which. In these instances you will get a chance to show that you are a manager with "bottle".

If the problem is severe enough that it is affecting the quality of the work or the other people in the group, you will need to confront the issue and attempt to find a solution. You will need to be firm but fair, to try to see things from the other person's point of view — but keep in mind that you are the manager and you have a responsibility to your team and the organisation to sort out the problem. You need to be clear and consistent in how you approach the problem, and ensure that you communicate concisely what needs to happen to resolve the issue.

To be an effective manager, however, you will need to be careful not to get in a situation where you have favourites and non-favourites. Obviously you will get along better with some people than with others, but your responsibility is to get good work out of all members of your team, not just those you like best. A client of mine in the brewery industry was so concerned about not appearing to have favourites that she recorded the amount of time she spent with each member of her team to be sure that it was the same for all. One-to-one meetings, quarterly reviews, etc. all lasted for exactly the same length of time for each. She said that of the eight people who reported to her, two were distinctly unlikeable and this disciplined approach was her way of ensuring that she was fair to each.

The Fun Factor

In any organisation, but especially one under pressure, it is essential that people enjoy themselves as well. Having a laugh, celebrating great results, organising social events can all help to defuse tense situations and release pressure of overworked staff. Generally speaking, people do work hard and as a manager it is your responsibility to see that they enjoy themselves as well.

Leadership and the Art of Delegation

Two crucial aspects of managing your team are leadership and delegation. To be a truly effective manager you need to inspire and give direction to your team, and you also need to know how and when to delegate to team members. Because these issues are so important, separate chapters will be devoted to each.

Chapter Five

THE ART OF DELEGATION

Delegation is an absolutely vital management skill, yet many managers do it poorly or not at all. But with organisations continuing to shed layers of management in an effort to be "lean and mean", it is more important than ever that the remaining managers learn how to get maximum productivity from themselves and their staff — and that means the art of delegation.

I frequently discuss delegation with my clients and am amazed at how often I hear them say that they are the only ones who can do a particular job or some new initiative — even when they are also complaining about how overburdened they are and how they need to reduce their workload! In many cases, they are on an ego trip or else feel that they need to justify their salaries by working themselves to the bone. But remember: good management is about getting things done and getting good work out of your staff — and delegation is the key to both.

In this chapter we will explore the many benefits of delegation: what it can do for you as a manager and how it can help to develop your team. We will look at the reasons why people don't delegate and suggest a proven method for delegating effectively and pain- lessly. Finally, we will discuss how delegation can be measured and what can be learned from this.

What Delegation Will Do for You

The primary benefit of delegation for you is clearly that it will free up your time for other things. Many manag- ers today feel that they are under ever-increasing time pressures (see Chapter Two, "Managing Your Time") and a failure to delegate is a definite contributor to this problem. Many first-time managers, in particular, fail to make the transition from "doing" to "managing" and try to continue handling activities themselves that would be better handled by others.

Well-planned delegation will give you more time to focus on the key issues facing the group or organisa- tion, more time to develop your leadership talents, and more time to devote to personal or family matters. Above all, it will enable you to concentrate on the issues that allow you to provide real value to the or- ganisation.

Delegation will also be useful in determining your team members' strengths and weaknesses. By giving individuals increased tasks and responsibilities, you will find out what they are capable of, who is likely to rise in the organisation, and so on. Delegation is thus a key skill for any successful manager.

What Delegation Will Do for Your Team

Well-handled delegation also has obvious benefits for people who report to you. They will feel that they are trusted, that they are an important part of the team, and that they will have new challenges and opportunities to prove what they can do. It also helps them to become more self-confident and to enjoy their work. If poorly handled, of course, delegation can lead to frustration and can damage self-confidence, but later in the chapter we'll look at the proper way to delegate.

Why People Don't Delegate

The primary reason managers don't delegate as much as they should is that they don't think their staff are up to the job. This, of course, then becomes a self-fulfilling prophesy as staff members become bored and demotivated and the quality of their work suffers.

I once had a very capable client with a bright future who, when asked to give examples of his delegation in the last year, could only come up with a handful. He basically said that he set very high standards and felt that they wouldn't be met if he delegated important tasks to others. He could delegate when he was away on holidays, or when the workload simply became too great, but as a rule would delegate only when he absolutely had to. I told him that his attitude was unacceptable and that it would hinder his progress in the organisation. Indeed, I told him that he was being selfish and that he would never grow as a manager if he didn't learn the skill of delegation. He eventually agreed and we worked out a plan, which is the basis for the next section on how to delegate.

The attitude shown by the manager above is unfortunately not unusual. Many managers simply don't see delegation as an important skill, and even those who claim that they take it seriously do not approach it in a professional and consistent way. Perhaps they feel a need to take personal responsibility for key tasks, or that they don't want to burden their staff with difficult work, or that they are somehow shirking responsibility by delegating jobs to others. If so, they are mistaken and don't understand what being a manager is all about.

Delegation does not mean relinquishing authority or avoiding responsibility — indeed, quite the opposite. And to repeat a point made in the previous chapter: the most important resource you have is the people who work for you and the way to get the best from them is through sensible and carefully planned and monitored delegation.

What and How to Delegate

Once you have decided to make a concerted effort to delegate more of your work, you should look in your diary at the activities over the next six to eight weeks to see which could be delegated. Perhaps you won't delegate the entire task but only a part of it, which in itself is a key aspect of delegating. You might delegate smaller tasks, such as developing an administrative process which will help to ensure that departmental meetings happen at the optimum periods in the year; or you might delegate major projects that will help specific staff members to develop and gain experience. The point is that, as a manager, it is up to you to decide what gets delegated and to whom.

Another very simple, ongoing approach to delegation is to refrain from solving every problem and answering every question yourself. If one of your staff members says to you, "We've got a problem, could you come down and give us some advice," you should stop and consider before doing so. Although you most likely could solve the problem for them, a far better course of action might be to ask them to come up with alternatives themselves. Otherwise, they could become too dependent on your expertise and experience and not develop any of their own. If you ask them to identify alternatives, recommend a course of action and then defend it, you are doing far more for them than just solving the current problem.

If you follow the above advice, you will not only find that you have more time to concentrate on other matters — rather than spending time yourself putting out fires — but that eventually your team is able to solve problems without bringing them to you in the first place. Now that's good management!

The Importance of Clear Communication

Obviously when delegating it is important that you are very clear in your briefing. It is not fair to the person to whom you are delegating if they are not absolutely certain what is expected of them and when. When delegation is not successful, poor communication is almost always at the root of the problem.

One of my clients has developed a simple system for delegation that is followed religiously in her company. It consists of two distinct parts: the initial briefing and follow-up dates for review.

Initial Briefing

During the initial briefing, all aspects of the task are discussed until there is a complete understanding of what is required. It is then written up and copied to both parties so that there won't be any confusion about the details at a later date. In particular, the manager delegating needs to be clear on what questions will be asked on the follow-up review dates. The staff member will then know exactly what is expected, and both will feel confident about the process. At the end of the meeting, review dates will be agreed, though the manager needs to emphasise that if anything unexpected and important occurs before then, it should be highlighted and discussed immediately.

Progress Review Meetings

This is the key to successful delegation. It is important for both parties that progress be reviewed at regular dates so that any problems or questions can be addressed at that time. The person performing the delegated task or project cannot just be left to "get on with it" — to sink or swim on their own — but instead needs reassurance that they are on the right track. If there are no problems or questions, or if the person is clearly on top of the situation, the follow-up meetings might be short and to the point. But they still need to happen.

And, as a manager, it is clearly your responsibility to know the status of the project you have delegated, as well as how your staff member is coping with the responsibility given to them. By scheduling these regular review meetings, and by telling the staff member what information you will require, you will be telling them that you are giving them added responsibility but will help them as needed to deal with it.

The Benefits of Delegation

Let's just review the positive things that happen if you follow the above approach to delegating:

- You will be able to attend to other business knowing that that particular task is being handled and that you will be able to review its progress.

- You will know that you are helping a staff member to develop and grow by giving them added responsibility, while at the same time giving them support as needed.

- The person to whom you have delegated will feel confident that they have been trusted with the task, that they have a full understanding of the brief, that they have agreed to the review dates and know the key questions that will be discussed, and that they will get assistance if they run into difficulties.

- Finally, by delegating in this way you will get invaluable information about the capabilities of your staff. You will know who can be given even more responsibility and who might need additional coaching or training.

Evaluating Delegation

At the end of a project, it is advisable that you sit down together and review how the whole process went. You can discuss what problems occurred, whether milestones were met, what could have gone better, and so on. You can evaluate the staff member on their initiative and creativity, on the quality of their decision-making and on how they handled responsibility. You can also ask them how they viewed the project, what they found especially difficult, and how you could have been of more assistance if there had been problems. You will thus learn a great deal about those working for you.

After you have reviewed the project you can then identify the key strengths and weaknesses displayed by the staff member, and discuss together how to build on the former and improve on the latter.

Delegation Minefields

Although the benefits of delegation should now be apparent, it is by no means always easy to do. Some people take to delegation very well and some simply do not want the challenge or responsibility. Some may try to do too much, and others will only do part of it and lean on you for direction and confirmation. Some may be a bit lazy and others simply lack confidence. In all cases, however, you need to follow the advice above and show your steel as a manager. Make sure that your staff do what they agreed to and don't accept excuses or shoddy work.

You also need to be careful about those who delegate their work on to others. If that happens, be sure your staff member is able to answer all questions put to them and is on top of the project. Let them know that it is *their* responsibility, and that if you had wanted someone else to handle it you would have delegated it to that person. On the other hand, it is possible that your staff member has learned from you very well and has become adept at the art of delegation!

Delegate and Give Space

One of my clients took to delegating as a key component of his management style and followed the advice given in this chapter. His one failing, however, was that he could not then leave his people alone to get on with the task. He thought that he was being supportive and was making himself available for advice or assistance. In reality, though, his staff felt that he did not trust them and became frustrated at his constant interference in their work. Eventually it became clear that there was a serious problem and, to my client's credit, he realised that the problem was with him. He was then able to restrict his input to the progress meetings and any emergency situations, and both he and his team benefited considerably.

Delegating for Promotion

A final word on delegation: it can be an extremely useful tool in identifying the high flyers on your team, even your possible successor. You may want to discuss it with your boss first, but by delegating very important tasks to a key individual, you can prepare the way for a future leader of the group. This kind of delegation needs to be very carefully considered — for example, you need to be careful not to create tension and resentment among the rest of the staff — but if handled properly will help to identify managers of the future.

Chapter Six

MANAGING UPWARDS

Managing upwards is a critical, but often undervalued, management skill. Your immediate boss is of considerable importance to you, not only because of his direct impact on your job duties and remuneration, but also because of his influence on your reputation throughout the organisation. How you are perceived by others — your strengths and weaknesses, your potential in the organisation, your personal qualities — all stem to a large degree from your boss's views. Your relationship with your boss is thus of critical importance to your success in the organisation.

Managing upwards is not about politics. It is not about dreaming up ways to impress your boss, or scheming to have some rival undermined so you will advance. It is another management skill based on acute observation, an understanding of company strategy and common sense. Developing a strong sustained relationship with your boss is your responsibility, however. It is not up to your boss — who presumably has pressures of his own — and it certainly can't be left to chance. Without it being planned and managed, your accomplishments, and the accomplishments of those working for you, may go unnoticed and unappreciated — with all that that implies.

This chapter explores different ways to ensure effective management of your boss. It looks at issues of communication, loyalty and empathy. It addresses ways of getting to know your boss, understanding his needs and taking appropriate action. It will also look at situations where a poor relationship has developed and consider various ways of rectifying the situation.

Communication

Clear communication is a prerequisite for managing upwards effectively. In particular, you will need to have a clear understanding of what your boss expects from you. I've worked with several clients who have expressed concern in this area. I have suggested that they say to their boss: "At the end of the day, how will you be measuring me, not specifically but in overall terms?" The response you get should help you understand what your boss is looking for, and therefore what you need to communicate to him.

Your boss clearly does not want to be burdened with every aspect of your job — and giving too much information will make you look disorganised, unsure of your priorities and unsure of yourself. So in your three-hour thinking sessions (see Chapter 2) consider carefully which issues you should communicate to your boss and which you should not. Whatever you decide, prioritise them and make sure that the really important ones get through. Be sure also to include issues that could have any impact on the effectiveness or reputation of your boss. These may be difficult to express, but express them you must to avoid being disloyal or even duplicitous. Once you have decided on all the key issues you need to convey to your boss, be sure that you are fully informed on each and follow up as needed. Avoid sending important information at the last minute — even if you are uncertain, you need to communicate what you know or don't know as soon as possible.

When communicating a problem to your boss it is crucial that you have thought it through carefully and are able to suggest one or two possible solutions. This will show that you are on top of the situation and, even if your boss doesn't agree with your recommendations, your efforts are likely to be noticed and appreciated.

Note, however, that there is a fine balance between keeping too close to your boss and not being close enough. I had a client who was committed to giving his boss every support possible. He came back from a week's holiday and found that there were no major issues or problems to report to his boss, whom he knew was extremely busy. After a few days he received a sarcastic phone message asking, "Have you returned from holidays yet?" My client immediately telephoned to explain why he had not made contact, but no doubt some damage had already been done. There is a lesson there about communication, but also about the topic of the next section.

Know Your Boss Well

Everyone has their strong points and weak points, and as a manager you should be aware of — and make use of — your boss's own personality traits. For example, is he a morning person or an afternoon person? When is the best time to have serious discussions or ask sensitive questions? Does he like a lot of detailed information, or does he prefer just to hear the basics? Learn to read your boss's moods. If he has just come from a stressful meeting it's probably not the right time to bring up a problem you're having. You may need to be flexible and patient, but you are far more likely to get positive results if you are sensitive to your boss's state of mind at all times.

In managing your boss, it is helpful to try to anticipate his needs whenever possible. For example, I had a client who was aware that her boss made numerous presentations and asked if there was anything she could do to help. She then got involved in preparing charts and other materials which was very helpful to her boss. After each presentation she would enquire if there was anything that could be improved which led to several innovative changes. By showing some initiative and common sense, she had made a very positive impression on her boss.

Developing a Relationship

In the same way that you need to ensure regular one-to-one meetings with those reporting to you, so must you meet with your boss on a personal basis. You need to set an agenda for these meetings and make it clear that you find them invaluable. It is your responsibility to make sure that these meetings are productive and useful for both you and your boss. Remember: this is an ideal opportunity to make a positive impression and to prove your value to the organisation.

One of my clients recently came to me complaining that his boss had no understanding or appreciation of the work he was doing. He went on and on saying that everything was his boss's fault until I finally raised my hand and said, "Enough. Unless you take responsibility for putting things right they never will be. Now let's find a way of tackling this which will meet the needs of both you and your boss." We then came up with the Two Pager report (see Chapter 3) which worked re-markably well in solving his problem.

Basically, whether you like or dislike your boss is ir-relevant. They are not there to be liked but to be effec-tive, just as you are. It is up to you to find a way of working with your boss that is beneficial for both of you and for the organisation.

Perceptions

The importance of perceptions has already been discussed, and it is obviously crucial to be aware of how
you are perceived by your boss. In fact, this issue is so
important that I would advise you to follow the practice of one of my clients in this regard. At every annual
review, after the formal performance appraisal has
been completed, she asks for an off-the-record discussion of how she is perceived by those in power. She is
careful to keep her mouth shut and just to listen, and
above all not to get defensive or try to explain herself.
She is aware that it doesn't matter whether what her
boss says is fair or accurate, it is how she is *perceived*
that is important and she has to work on that perception. Overall, she finds that the discussion is extremely
useful to her personally, and that it also tends to make
her boss want to help her to improve on how she is
perceived in the organisation. This makes it a very important part of managing upwards.

If you are not convinced that perceptions are important, here are some words and phrases I've heard
used by senior managers to describe people working
for them:

- "Naïve"

- "Immature"

- "Gets up people's noses at meetings"

- "Tries too hard to please"

- "Always has to be right"

- "Always has to have the last word", and so on.

Now it is these kinds of perceptions that can mean that people don't get promoted or given important assignments. And they are the kind of comments you would possibly never hear or be aware of — unless you ask for an honest, off-the-record opinion from your boss or other influential people in the organisation.

Managing how you are perceived can be very difficult and even unpleasant. You may not relish being told that you are naïve — as I was told when I was thirty — and your response might be to get angry or to bury your head in the sand. But remember that you are always learning and that you can always make improvements. Instead of getting angry, be grateful that you have something concrete to work on and get on with the business of changing those negative perceptions.

Learn from Your Staff

One strategy for managing upwards is to think very carefully about how you want your staff to operate, and then try to do the same for your boss. I had one client who took the process of managing upwards very seriously and put a great deal of thought into it. She decided to look at her own team to see how she would like them to operate. Here is what she decided:

- She wanted them to initiate things themselves without constantly asking for permission.

- She wanted them to take on more responsibilities so that she had time to think about bigger issues.

- She wanted reports to be on time, memos and e-mails to be answered promptly without her having to chase for them.

- She wanted her team to think through possible solutions to problems before they came to her.

- She wanted people to be able to read her moods and understand when she was under pressure, etc.

- She wanted her team to be mature, to use their common sense and to focus on the important issues facing them.

With this list in hand she went to her boss and had a very fruitful discussion about how she could support him better.

Handle Your Boss with Care

Two final bits of advice on managing upwards: always be loyal to your boss and never try to outshine him.

Being loyal to your boss primarily means not going behind their back when things aren't going your way. I had a client once who felt that he was being badly treated by his boss and, instead of discussing it with him, decided to go over his head to a board director.

My client was sacked. The stark fact is that, in most cases, you need to learn how to deal with your boss and should avoid undermining their position by going behind their back.

Finally, be careful not to make yourself look good at your boss's expense. It is natural to want to get the credit for high quality work or ideas, but it is generally a good idea to be sure that your boss reaps some of the rewards as well. You do not want your boss to feel threatened or intimidated by your accomplishments, as that will most likely lead to difficulties at a later stage. If your work is first-rate — and even though your boss might get more credit than is deserved — you will eventually receive the accolades and advancement you deserve.

Managing Sideways

Before moving on to the next chapter, it is worthwhile noting briefly the importance of managing sideways as well as upwards. With the increasing pressures imposed on managers today, it is useful to build bridges with colleagues or peers, as well as with certain contacts outside the organisation. By doing so, you are laying foundations for future support when needed, as well as obtaining useful guidance and information. There will be times when you need to get assistance from your peers in the organisation, and it will only be forthcoming if you have spent some time building strong relationships beforehand.

Chapter Seven

MANAGING WITH INTEGRITY

Integrity — noun "1. adherence to moral principles; honesty. 2. the quality of being unimpaired;
soundness. 3. unity; wholeness." (*Collins Concise
English Dictionary*)

The astute reader will not be surprised that I view this
as a key chapter in the book. Indeed, I would argue that
managing with integrity is essential to achieving success without selling your soul. In recent years, there
have been many books written on business ethics —
thanks to countless scandals and bad business practices
— and any organisation needs to consider carefully
whether it operates in an ethical way. In this chapter,
however, the focus will primarily be on personal integrity — in other words, on the values that guide you as a
manager.

Managers face ethical dilemmas nearly every day of
their working lives. And because they are in a position
of power, they need to be particularly sensitive to the
impact their decisions have on others. Among the many
areas where ethical issues can arise are:

- Equality in the workplace

- Right to privacy

- Working conditions

- Insider dealing

- Conflict of interest

- Sexual harassment

- Corruption and bribery

- Price-fixing and unfair competition

- Unsafe products

- Etc., etc.

Obviously, the above list represents only the tip of the iceberg, but the point is that managers have a heavy burden in terms of ethical choices in the workplace. Fortunately, many organisations now take ethics seriously and have policies in place on how to deal with various dilemmas that arise, and of course many of the issues in the above list have legal ramifications as well. But many ethical issues fall into a somewhat grey area and the successful manager needs to operate using their own sense of integrity.

I have discussed the subject of integrity with numerous people over the years and have included many of their views in the pages that follow. The intent here is to understand what qualities — both positive and negative — are associated with integrity and to examine why managing with integrity is *always* the best option. As a manager you need to always be aware of the impact of integrity — integrity in managing yourself, integrity in managing your team and your boss, and integrity in managing the balance between work life and home life.

Integrity in the Organisation

Managing with integrity has taken on increased significance in recent years as tiers of management are removed from organisations and individuals are given more responsibility. People are expected to use their initiative and to make decisions, but they are also expected to get results. If they do not have a strong natural sense of integrity — a "moral compass" that can guide them — they can be tempted to cut corners or take advantage of people in the mistaken belief that that is the way to get ahead. They couldn't be more wrong.

Integrity should run right through the organisation, from the very top to the lowest rung. It needs to be part of the company's culture so that every individual knows what is expected of them and how they should behave. There needs to be open and honest communication, and a climate of trust should be preached and practised throughout the organisation. People need to know that they can make and admit to mistakes, that they are accountable for their actions but will be treated fairly at all times.

The difficulty comes, naturally enough, in organisations that do not take the above approach. There are some organisations that foster a success-at-any-cost culture that worries about the bottom line first and ethics and morals last, if at all. The integrity-conscious manager often will have great difficulty in such organisations and my only advice would be to consider alternatives. Whatever the situation, do not succumb to the temptations to operate in a less than ethical way — it will most likely catch up with you and is not a healthy way to live. In any case, it is completely unnecessary.

Various Views on Integrity

It is clear that integrity means different things to different people, and below is a wide range of views on how various people think of integrity. When added together, they present an interesting picture of what it means to manage with integrity.

- One contact of mine claims that he just has a strong overall sense of what integrity is and knows when he is turning away from it. He sees life as a series of jumps, and knows that he can go around one but that the next one will be even higher. The more he avoids issues where he should be true to himself and take the jump, the greater the chance of disaster striking later. He now makes a point of watching for jumps and trying to take them on the first time.

- For another client, self-respect is the key. She feels that she has to set a good example to those working for her and to treat them fairly at all times. Working at self-respect gives her the confidence to tackle anything that is thrown at her.

- Another client sees trustworthiness as key to his attitude towards integrity, particularly in terms of confidentiality. All one-to-one discussions of sensitive matters are kept absolutely confidential to avoid whispering in the corridors of the company.

- Openness in relationships is considered the defining factor for another client. She goes out of her way to ensure that all members of her team know how they are viewed and are told when things are going badly or well. Without openness, she argues, there can be no trust.

- Another client refuses to accept double standards in his team — mainly because he was a victim of them early in his career. He is very conscious of treating his boss, his peers and his staff members in the same way and with the same standards applying to each.

- One of my clients says that being incorruptible is his main reaction to integrity. He is in a business where slush funds can easily appear and is determined to avoid even an appearance of any impropriety. He even double checks his expense accounts to ensure that they are accurate and fair.

- The views of several of my clients have been shaped by experiences they've had earlier in their careers. For example, one feels very strongly that loyalty to your boss and to your team members is very important. He once had a team member go behind his back which caused all kinds of problems. He now does everything he can to promote a sense of loyalty in his group.

- Another client views "being responsible" as the key to integrity. By that she means not passing the buck when things go wrong, which she used to be guilty of and realised that her team members thought less of her for it. She now freely admits it when she makes a mistake and feels relieved that she does not have to try to be perfect.

- One of my clients makes the point that it is more difficult to act with integrity when things are going well and you're on the fast track in the organisation. He says that there can be a temptation to cut corners, or to take advantage of people at such times, even if you are likely to act with integrity when things go wrong.

- Another client argues that having "bottle" is the key to integrity. By "bottle" he means being true to oneself, not avoiding issues, facing adversity when required to do so. He will not allow tough times or bad luck to be an excuse for not acting with integrity.

- One client says that refusing to tell "white lies" — for example, fudging the expense account — is a sign of integrity. He argues that a lack of integrity in managing the small things could easily lead to the same in more important areas.

- Other clients say that integrity is about not being arrogant; or not being boastful or selfish; or that it is about not being inconsistent or unpredictable.

- Integrity is about not being deceitful. One of my clients became involved in an office romance and felt compelled to lie about it to keep it hidden. He had always prided himself on his honesty and this affair severely damaged his reputation.

The Importance of Character

No doubt you will draw your own conclusions from the various views on integrity listed above, but underlying most of them seems to be the importance of moral courage. This means having the courage to be true to your own beliefs and values, and refusing to take a seemingly more expedient route for short-term success. This kind of moral courage is part and parcel of your overall character, but that doesn't mean that you can't work and improve on it. Above all, you need to be aware of the moral choices you make almost every day in the workplace and at home.

Integrity When Managing Yourself

If you look back at the opening chapter on "Managing Yourself", you will see that many of the characteristics described there reflect back to integrity: the importance of preparation; why you should welcome accountability; managing with "bottle"; developing a positive attitude; and making the most of adversity. To be an effective manager you need to be true to yourself and to endeavour to be the best you can be. But you also need to acknowledge those areas where you are not strong and not beat yourself up for not being perfect. Accept that you will always have much to learn and welcome advice from your boss, peers and staff members. It takes integrity and moral courage to admit to failings and weaknesses, but it will make you a better manager in the long run.

Integrity When Managing Your Team

Integrity here often means setting a good example. Your team will look to you for guidance and leadership and if you fail to manage with integrity it will cascade down through the group. If you cut corners or take advantage of people, they will assume that they should as well. Even your personal behaviour could have a major impact on your team. I remember one married client who was having an affair with one of his managers in a fairly public way. Everyone knew that after each meeting he was rushing off to meet her, and he eventually lost the respect of his staff. His own performance also suffered and within months he was sacked.

Managing with integrity means being firm but fair. You should listen to other viewpoints and encourage participation, but also be seen as decisive and consistent. You want to be approachable so that a staff member can come to you with a problem, but you don't want to become so buddy-buddy that you have difficulty offering constructive criticism or maintaining discipline. As with so much of managing, integrity involves balance and fairness. And at all times you need to remember that your team will be greatly affected by your personal integrity.

Integrity When Managing Your Boss

As discussed in the chapter on "Managing Upwards", integrity in this case means showing loyalty to your boss and not going behind his back. I remember a client who decided his boss wasn't up to scratch. Without giving any warning to his boss he went to a senior director to express his views. The director listened patiently before showing the manager out, and within two months my client was looking for a new job. He learned a valuable lesson about integrity when managing your boss.

Of course, there could be times when your boss does not deserve your loyalty. For example, if you believe that your boss is behaving in an unethical or illegal manner, you have a responsibility to speak up. Obviously much would depend on the details and circumstances, and in all cases you would need to consider your options carefully, but standing by idly is obviously not an option in terms of integrity. You need to be as sure as possible that your suspicions are justified, and then decide whether you should take it to a director or someone else to deal with.

Integrity When Managing the Balance with Your Home Life

As discussed earlier, being a whole manager — and thus one with integrity — means taking into account the needs and concerns of yourself, your partner and family. Far too many managers today feel under pressure in the workplace and allow their home life to come a distant second in terms of their time or concern. Don't let this happen to you. Life is too short to spend all your time on the job, thus ignoring your partner or failing to see your children growing up.

This problem of balance can occur when things are going well *and* when they are going badly. If they're going well the manager feels that they're a high-flyer and wants to devote even more time to the job. They are getting great praise and a sense of self-worth at work and either take their home life for granted or ignore it altogether. When things are going poorly, the manager feels that they need to work even harder to get things on track. They may feel somewhat inadequate in the job, which can spill over into their home life, or else they try to shelter their partner altogether from the difficulties at work. Either way, estrangement often results.

Never underestimate the importance of actively working on the balance. I once had a very successful client who came to realise that he was in serious trouble in terms of his family and resolved to do something about it. He devised a series of actions to address the problem. First of all, he decided that he would treat his wife much as he would a key customer. He no longer took her for granted, was courteous and respectful, and rarely said things he would regret later. He also suggested that they have scheduled meetings every two months to discuss how things were between them and how they could improve their partnership. Out of these meetings, it transpired that his wife wanted to go back to college for a degree and he was able to help her with the arrangements. For other family members, he gave specific responsibilities to them for various projects, such as where they would go on their next holiday, whether it was possible to build an extension onto the house, and so on. Gradually, he was able to repair the damage he had done earlier and was once again fully involved with his family.

Your integrity reflects who you are — what kind of person you are and what kind of values you have. Whether your integrity stems from religious beliefs, family upbringing, personal philosophy or whatever, you need to be aware of it at all times and be conscious of how your decisions reflect on yourself and others.

In my view, integrity consists of three fundamental characteristics: honesty, responsibility and courage. But however you define it, the fact is that achieving success without integrity is a hollow accomplishment indeed — and one that is unlikely to lead to contentment in the long term.

Chapter Eight

LEADERSHIP

Leadership is a topic that has been discussed, debated and written about since history began. There are a great number of leaders who have proved that they could influence and inspire others to achieve great things. One definition of leadership that I particularly like is that "a leader is a person followed by others". I think that that strikes at the heart of the matter.

A leader can also be viewed as someone who gets the best out of the people they influence — in terms of the organisation's objectives and goals as well as their own personal potential. But in business, leadership is also linked to the bottom line. Few organisations will reward leaders who fail to achieve the financial results on which companies need to survive.

In this chapter, we will look at why leadership is important and what makes an effective leader. We will look at leadership in both good times and bad, and consider whether every manager should aspire to be a leader. Finally, we will look at leadership in the context of managing oneself, managing one's boss and team, and in managing the balance — in other words, how leadership relates to becoming a whole manager.

Why is Leadership Needed?

As has been noted earlier, business organisations are undergoing greater pressures than ever before and these seem likely to continue for the foreseeable future. Shareholders are becoming more demanding, government and the media more intrusive, employees more aware of their rights, competition more intense, and cataclysmic changes seemingly occur daily. The increasing flow of information means that solutions to problems and exploiting opportunities need to happen more quickly and effectively. There is less and less time for directors to direct and managers to manage, which means that both groups need to develop their leadership skills to influence people to make things happen — which, incidentally, is another good definition of leadership.

In fact, as more organisations become global and competition intensifies, leaders need to be developed at all levels of the organisation. One of my clients, who holds a top job in the European operation of a global company, is responsible for a new initiative searching for potential leaders in divisions throughout Europe. He has realised that successful implementation of their complex business strategy will not happen without people with leadership skills. Developing training programmes on leadership is now one of their top priorities.

The Key Elements of Leadership

Leadership is obviously a big subject and we will not attempt to cover every facet of it here. There are numerous books available on leadership and I would urge the reader to refer to them for additional information. Instead, I will try to focus on the key elements of leadership that I have experienced in my career and with my clients.

A client and I decided to define our sense of leadership and came up with a somewhat wordy definition:

> "Leadership is the ability and will to influence men and women in such a way as to ensure their commitment to achieve, and includes a strength of character which inspires confidence."

In rather more elegant terms, leaders should know where they are going and how they are going to get there, and be able to communicate to others in a way that makes it happen. They should have the capacity to take the initiative, to make decisions and be fully accountable for the results. Leaders welcome − even relish − responsibility and tend to have considerable faith in their own abilities and judgement.

People who are not leaders tend to avoid making decisions in the hope that problems will go away. They are more likely to accept the status quo and are fearful of "rocking the boat" or taking risks.

Leaders are prepared to fly alone like eagles and not to look for the comfort or safety of the easy option.

They are willing to be uncomfortable at times, to make decisions that are unpopular and to live with the consequences.

Another important facet of leadership is the ability to see the big picture, to rise above the minutiae of day-to-day work to understand the broader goals of the organisation. Leaders are able to see the whole picture, and not just their own smaller part in it.

Finally, a leader needs to learn to stand up and be counted, even if their view goes against the wishes or goals of others in the organisation. Obviously, a leader must pick and choose their battles carefully, must know when to dig in their heels and when it makes more sense to compromise, but leadership does involve taking a stand when it matters and being true to oneself.

Leadership in Fair Weather

Most people assume that it is easier to show leadership qualities when things are going well, that when there are fewer pressures one has time to focus on managing others. In my experience, it is often during good times that problems start to emerge.

I know a company director with excellent leadership qualities who says that she is always particularly vigilant when things are going well. For example, she would conduct an unexpected performance assessment with key players to identify what was going well and what could be going better. In this way, she guards against complacency and lack of focus for her team to ensure that standards don't slip. Now this approach takes "bottle", because she could be introducing some discomfort where there was none before — but then, as we've seen, "bottle" is an important part of leadership.

It is also easy to become smug and self-congratulatory when things are going well — which also can be a recipe for disaster. I have another client, who is a very good leader, who says that he always keeps in mind that it is the strength of the brand that brings him success, not just his own efforts. In that way he keeps his feet on the ground and doesn't allow himself to get carried away during the good times.

Leadership When Times are Tough

Most people agree that the test of a good leader is when the going gets rough. Such occasions concentrate the mind and encourage focus on key issues while less important ones are put on the back burner where they belong. It is a good time to observe effective leaders and to learn from them.

A company I worked for launched a new product where the main objective was to obtain wide distribution in different types of outlets. One of the regions started badly and it became clear that the regional manager had made serious mistakes in his planning and communication to his team. He was severely criticised.

When he realised that things were not right he called in his team, discussed the situation with each of his managers and agreed new distribution targets. He then spent time with each manager discussing their specific strategies for reaching the new targets, making his own suggestions and comments as needed. He then arranged for daily "phone-ins" from each so that he could monitor the progress and discuss any necessary changes. Eventually, the situation started to improve.

This manager showed definite leadership qualities on this occasion. He accepted blame and responsibility for the situation, and had the bottle to go back to the drawing board to devise a new strategy. He was prioritised, exhibited good communication skills, showed that he trusted his people, but he expected results.

In adversity, leaders should stay calm, show a readiness to listen and take on board sound advice, yet be resolute when necessary. It is a time to learn what you are made of, and afterwards you should take note of what went well or poorly to log away for future use if needed.

Leadership When Managing Yourself

Clearly a leader must have the qualities described in the opening chapter — must be prepared and organised, a good manager of time, have plenty of "bottle", see the glass as half-full rather than half-empty, and so forth. Indeed, a leader will excel in all those areas.

I once had a very ambitious client who was determined to become a Vice President (at least!) in his company. I was somewhat concerned by this ambition, as he appeared to me as unlikely material for a leadership role. He was not prioritised, he was indecisive, he was even somewhat unkempt in his appearance. We discussed this and he was very taken aback to hear that he was perceived in this way by his colleagues, his team and myself as his executive coach. We then sat down to put together a plan aimed at developing him as a decisive, clear-thinking leader.

He was a very capable strategic thinker with a particular ability to visualise future trends. My advice centred on his becoming more articulate and authoritative, especially in meetings, and on improving his written documents. This strategy seemed to work as he soon developed increased self-confidence and conviction. He is now a Senior Vice President and has become a leading light in his organisation.

Leadership in Managing Your Team

This is the area where leadership — or the lack of it — is the most apparent. What does your team think of you? When you are on holiday or out of the office, what are they saying about you? Are they saying, "Well, he's a decent enough chap and is pretty easy to get along with"? If so, I'd say you have your work cut out for you. If instead they are saying, "My goodness, my boss is demanding, but at least she's clear about what she expects and what she's trying to achieve" — then I'd say you are exhibiting leadership qualities.

Leadership in managing your team is about being tough, but fair, about being very clear about what you are trying to achieve and what you expect of your team. Above all, it is about inspiring your team to perform as well as possible, to *want* to do their best.

Leadership When Managing Upwards

To consider applying leadership to your relationship with your boss may seem somewhat odd. But as noted previously, increased pressures at every level in the organisation means that managers at the higher echelons are looking for ways to spend more time focused on serious issues. This means that you have the opportunity to take on increased responsibility, while making sure that your actions have the genuine support of your boss.

One example that I remember involved one of my clients whose boss suddenly received increased responsibilities which meant he had less time to offer support to his team. The team, which included my client, became increasingly isolated and demotivated. My client realised that the situation could not continue, went to his boss and requested a meeting with the entire team to discuss the topic of "team motivation". His boss asked him if there was a serious problem, to which my client replied in the affirmative, and the boss said fine, let's have a meeting and get everything into the open. The meeting was a considerable success and everyone benefitted.

This is a good example of leadership in managing upwards and, considering the response from the boss, a good example of leadership in managing your team as well. The qualities shown included identifying the problem, having the bottle to address it, using good communication skills and good follow-up.

Personal Qualities of a Leader

What are the personal qualities that you find in a manager who is clearly a leader? What kind of person are they likely to be? I prepared such a list for one of my clients and reproduce it below:

- Someone who knows where they are going and how they are going to get there — has leadership qualities.

- Someone who understands the need to involve others — delegates well and knows how to get people on their side.

- Someone who is seen to have authority.

- Someone who makes decisions easily and is decisive in general.

- Someone who is well organised and understands how to prioritise their time.

- Someone who is in control of their emotions.

- Someone with a level of self-confidence but not arrogance and who has a positive outlook — one who sees the bottle as half-full, not half-empty.

You may want to add to or change the above list, but for me it represents a clear description of a leader who gets things done. As an exercise, you might rate yourself on a scale of one to ten on each of the above points. The marks — assuming you've been true to yourself! — should reveal what you have to work on to become an effective leader. Do not be disappointed if your marks are not as high as you would like. Consider it an opportunity for improvement — though you will need to do a fair amount of work.

Let's look at each of the points individually:

- *Someone who knows where they are going and how they are going to get there — has leadership qualities.*

Are you a leader? Somebody who thinks about the way to go forward, about what it will entail and how to go about achieving it? Or are you someone who waits for someone else to take the lead? Leadership is about setting goals and objectives, about monitoring your progress through various milestones, and about continually being mindful of others while you do so. It is an essential quality for all aspiring managers — you should start working on it today.

- *Someone who understands the need to involve others —
delegates well and knows how to get people on their side.*

All managers are essentially in the people business, and
building bridges with the people around you is a key
skill — not creaky bridges that will tip over under pressure but solid ones with a good strong foundation. Be
firm, flexible, fun, understanding, interested and interesting — these are all qualities which can make you the
kind of leader others will want to follow. Remember
that everyone is different, and that what motivates one
person might do the opposite for another. But be absolutely clear that to be a leader who gets things done, it
will be critical that you have the enthusiastic support
and assistance of those around you.

- *Someone who is seen to have authority.*

Are you someone who is good at making a speech,
talking at a meeting, writing a memo or letter, communicating in general? Here is a suggestion on how to
make an impact during a speech or while making a key
point at a meeting: get up, speak up, and shut up. Try
it, and see if it doesn't give a definite air of authority.
Avoid any procrastination, hesitancy, limp appearance
or behaviour, uncertainty, verbosity, etc. Be clear and
concise, yet don't forget to be interesting. And remember that appearance does matter. I once had a client
who was very well organised and an excellent speaker,
but his shirt was always rumpled, his tie was shoddy

and his overall appearance did him no favours. We had a frank discussion about it and eventually he agreed to radically alter his whole approach to great effect.

- *Someone who makes decisions easily and is decisive in general.*

This shows that you know where you stand on most issues and that you communicate it to others. Do not dither — if you don't know the answer or haven't yet formed an opinion on something, say so and indicate when you will decide. Whenever possible, make your decision, stick with it, and then move on to other things.

- *Someone who is well organised and understands how to prioritise their time.*

Being well organised may not sound all that difficult, yet we've all had the experience of working for people who are the opposite — completely disorganised and seemingly without priorities. Leaders have to know where they're going and how they're going to get there. They have to understand what really matters, which usually means using their three hour thinking sessions or some other mechanism for taking time to sort out their priorities.

- *Someone who is in control of their emotions.*

Leaders usually have the capacity to stay calm and in control during a crisis, and when things are normal they exude a quiet self-confidence. Leaders are able to use their intellect and reasoning to keep their emotions at bay. People who have difficulty controlling their emotions rarely make good leaders. Emotions are important — they are a vital part of being human — but they need to be channelled and managed to be an effective leader.

- *Someone with a level of self-confidence but not arrogance and who has a positive outlook — one who sees the bottle as half-full, not half-empty.*

Always work at developing a positive approach — always. There are many people who fall into the trap of always identifying the reasons why something *can't* be done. I had a client once who was very capable, intelligent and with strong problem-solving skills, but he would react negatively to almost any suggestion or idea. The solution I devised was for him to force himself to always follow a negative comment with a positive one. We followed this religiously and eventually he started to identify the positive points first. This does not mean that one should always be a "yes" person — only that it is a great virtue to approach any initiative with a positive mental attitude.

Chapter Nine

MANAGING YOUR CAREER

Given the amount of time one spends at work — and the importance of work to one's personal well-being — it is remarkable that so few people actually take the time to manage their career. This is not to say that it is possible to map out in advance every step you might take in your career, every department you may work in, every company you might work for, every position you might hold, and so forth. But it is possible — and indeed advisable — to ask yourself continually if your career is on the right track. Are you where you want to be and, if not, what are you going to do about it?

This chapter will address the issue of managing your career. It will look at the various work stages you are likely to go through in your career, and consider what questions you should be asking yourself in each. It will consider the advantages of the Three Career Options Approach and will look at the critical issues of finding a champion at work, using a network of key contacts and involving your family at every stage of the process.

It's Up to You

Anyone who expects their current organisation or anyone else to be responsible for their career path is either
naïve or delusional. The hard truth is that you are the
only one who has the ability and the self-interest to decide on what career path you choose. Your superiors
and colleagues could be of considerable assistance, as
we will see below, but the important point here is that
it is your responsibility, no one else's. In fact, I would
urge you to include your career progression and planning as one of the regular topics in your three-hour
quality thinking sessions, as described in Chapter 2.

In deciding on how to approach your career, as
usual it is best to keep the planning simple. One of my
clients spends a half-day every six months to focus ex-
clusively on her career. She takes a hard look at where
she's come from, where she is today and where she
would like to be in five or ten years. She then draws up
a plan for how she will reach her goals, including key
tasks with dates for each, and then transfers it to her
diary to ensure that she keeps to it. Obviously the plan
might change as situations arise, but the important
thing is to be actively managing the process so that you
are in control.

The approach needed today in managing your career will be considerably different to what it would
have been a generation ago. Whereas once it may have
been advisable to get a degree in a specialised disci-

pline from a top university and then look for life-long employment with regular promotions in a blue-chip company, the task facing today's aspiring manager is very different. Life-long employment in one company is now very unusual, and today's employees need a broad range of skills and experiences — as well as considerable flexibility — in order to achieve success. For the most part this is good news, as hard work and strong skills are more highly valued today than are background and where you came from. Career paths are much less straightforward than they once were, however, which is another argument for the importance of managing the process very carefully.

In looking at the career choices facing you, particularly in the early years, it is very important that you know yourself and are honest about your strengths and weaknesses. You need to know whether you'd be happier in a large company or a small one, a company that is highly structured or one that will give you considerable freedom, and so forth. That doesn't mean that you should rule out an option that is otherwise attractive, only that you need to be aware of situations that would suit you best.

If your heart is set on following a career in a particular area, make sure you take jobs in the early stages that give you the right kind of work experience — even if it means accepting a lower salary. At that stage, work experience is all-important and will provide the bedrock for the rest of your career. I have a good friend who has a high-level job in government after outstanding success in a number of key posts in industry. He places great emphasis on the fact that in the early days he took jobs that gave him a broad range of experience, which has proved invaluable to his success. He had the good sense to realise that work experience would be the key to later success.

Finally, remember that there is no one right career path and that it will vary greatly from individual to individual. A few might know what they want to do and how they would like to progress, but for most their careers will depend on a combination of skills, circumstances and a good bit of fortune. The key is to be true to yourself. Don't do things for the wrong reasons and, above all, approach your career with flexibility and a positive outlook.

Career Stages

This section looks at the various stages you are likely to go through in your career and the different choices to be made for each. Obviously the options — and concerns — for someone starting out in their career will be very different from those of someone who has been working for ten years, and very different again for someone contemplating retirement. Also, because every person is different, there is clearly no one right path or approach that will work for each individual. But in looking at the various stages of your career, there are certain questions you need to ask yourself. These questions will vary from person to person, but they might include:

- What do you want?

    ◊ Money?

    ◊ Recognition, fame?

    ◊ Self-fulfilment?

    ◊ A relaxed life?

- What sacrifices are you willing to make?

- What are your options?

- What are the pros and cons of each?

- What impact will your choice have on your partner or family?

- Do you have the "bottle" to do it?

Again, the above list may vary considerably and some points will carry much more weight than others. For example, if you know you are particularly risk-averse — or seriously ambitious — you need to factor that into the equation.

Below are the various career stages you are likely to experience.

First Employment

Many young people have no clear career in mind when they first enter the workforce. They may have taken a general liberal arts or business degree in university, or have no specific qualification and no idea what they would like to do. They are looking for the first step.

I am often asked by friends or clients to provide some career coaching for their sons or daughters and have devised a simple approach that seems to be very useful. I ask them to list on a piece of paper all the things they think they might like to do. This list should include any and all possible jobs in no particular order. I then ask them to select six which they think are feasible, again listed in any order. Next I ask them to take three of the six and list them in order of preference. Against these three serious possibilities, I ask them to list the actions they would need to take to make them happen. This might include doing further research, talking to people in those industries, taking temporary or part-time jobs in related fields, talking to human resource managers in specific companies, etc. The person then simply needs to act on each of the tasks and by doing so should acquire the information and experience needed to make an informed choice.

The key advice to anyone starting out is to remember that you are likely to go through many different positions and companies during your career and you need to be as open-minded and flexible as possible. The

key is to get as much experience as you can, to continually learn and increase your skills, and to maintain a
positive frame of mind.

First Five Years

After you have decided on a possible career to pursue
and have landed your first serious job, it is now time to
gain as much experience as possible. Ideally, you will
work for a company that has a well-thought-out training programme that will enable you to be exposed to
various aspects of the job, including computer training,
finance, marketing, management skills, etc. Your progress should be continually reviewed so that you
become aware of your strengths and any weaknesses. It
is also important at this stage — indeed, at every stage
— that you develop a good relationship with your immediate boss. As we have seen elsewhere in this book,
your boss is of critical importance in helping you grow
in the organisation.

During the first five years you may feel it necessary
to look around for other opportunities. It is always a
good idea to consider your options, particularly if you
do not feel you are making adequate progress or you
have serious concerns about your current position or
organisation. Having said that, it is essential that you
continue to show that you are prepared to do whatever
is necessary in your current job. You should always do
the best work you can in a professional manner so that
if you decide to make a change you will do so with the

right record behind you. That is key both to your career and to your self-confidence and continued success.

From Your Mid-20s to 40

Again, this could be a very important stage of your career as it will determine whether you are on the fast track, or whether you are likely to settle into a comfortable middle management role. You will need to take advantage of any opportunities available, such as studying for an MBA at your company's expense or gaining valuable work experience in another department or in an overseas office. As always, get as much experience and as many skills as possible, and have a frank discussion with your boss about how he or she sees your development. For some people, of course, they might be quite content with what they have achieved and not feel the need to strive for more. Be careful, however: in today's competitive work environment there is no room for complacency or standing still and you should always be looking to improve yourself.

From Age 40 to 55

By this stage, your career path should be fairly clear, though you still need to know how you are perceived by your boss and others in the organisation. Remember that there are typically three people or so in every organisation that have considerable influence and it is important that you are aware at all times of how they view you. At this stage you should also be particularly aware of your responsibility to those reporting to you. Are you helping them to progress in the organisation? Are you providing the kind of guidance and feedback that you received in the early stages of your career? Are you helping them to become whole managers?

From Age 55 to Retirement

There is a tendency now to retire earlier and live longer, so this stage is also very important. It is now time to think about how you will spend your retirement years and, in particular, how you might pass on the experience and knowledge you've gained. You might decide to do some consulting, or management coaching, or perhaps provide assistance to a local charity. Whatever you decide to do, at this stage you need to be preparing the groundwork by talking to your human resources department or managing director, by doing the necessary research and planning. And, as with all the previous stages, you need to be sure that you find the appropriate balance between your work life and home life and to consider your partner's wishes at all times.

The Three Options Career Approach

Another way to view your career is to always keep in mind that you have three basic options and to consider and be prepared for each. The three options that I see are (a) building on the status quo, (b) making a change, and (c) the "rainy day" option.

Building on the Status Quo

This option assumes that you are reasonably content with your position and organisation and that the main issues before you concern how to advance. The approach here is to follow much of the advice in this book: work closely with your boss, practise sound time management techniques, schedule regular three-hour quality thinking sessions, delegate well, and so on. Be aware of your strengths and weaknesses; build on the former and work on alleviating the latter.

Making a Change

This option assumes that you are not content with your current situation and need to consider making a change. Such a change might involve leaving your current organisation, or even possibly switching careers altogether. Whatever it is, you need to consider all the options carefully and go through your version of the list of questions that appeared earlier in this chapter. It is never easy making a major career change, but remember that *not* making a change is a decision as well and it is often preferable to plan carefully and then just do it.

The "Rainy Day" Option

This is the option that many people fail to consider, though I think that they should. Basically, this is the option that covers cataclysmic and unexpected change: losing your job, winning the lottery, having your company go under, whatever. Deciding how to spend your lottery winnings is probably not that difficult, but would you have a plan in mind for less attractive major upheavals? For example, would you consider self-employment if need be? If so, have you done any planning or research to prepare yourself for that possibility? Have you talked to people who are self-employed to get a sense of what it would take? The boy scout motto — *Be Prepared* — is very sensible advice indeed.

If you take the Three Options Career Choice you will know that you are doing the best you can in your current job, that you have considered what's involved in making a change, and that you have even made preparations should things go very wrong. This should help your self-confidence and peace of mind considerably, and convince yourself that you are managing your career with "bottle".

Outside Support

Throughout your career you will depend on the advice and support of various people. It is a truism that who you know can be as important as what you know, and you should endeavour at all times to cultivate and develop as many useful relationships as possible.

Involving Partners/Family

It is obviously important to include your partner and family in any major decision you make about your career. As noted elsewhere in this book, achieving a balance between work life and home life is critical in becoming a whole manager, and that means taking into consideration the views of those closest to you. That does not mean that you have to worry them unnecessarily with your planning for a "rainy day", but it does mean that you need to discuss your choices with them.

Internal Wise Men

Every organisation has in it men and women who are like nuggets of gold — valuable advisers who can help to steer you in the right direction. They typically have been around for a while, and though perhaps not particularly influential they know the business very well and can provide useful advice on how to approach your career. I was fortunate to have such a person at Unilever, a man who was extremely helpful to me.

Human Resource Managers/Managing Directors

Make a point of establishing a relationship with the HR Manager in a big company, or Managing Director in a smaller one, so that they know you are serious about developing your career. Ask them for advice on what you should do, what courses you should attend, what work experience you need, and so forth. They can be an invaluable resource — use them.

Executive Coaches

More and more people are looking to professional advisers who can help them make decisions about their careers. These people can help you identify your strengths and weaknesses, advise you on the options before you, help you to manage your boss better and much more.

Find a Champion

In large organisations in particular, it can be very useful to find someone to act as a champion on your behalf. For example, if you have a particularly good rapport with your boss, try to develop it further and nurture it, even if one of you is promoted and you no longer report to him. He can still be your champion, which means that he is working on your behalf in the corridors of power — helping to manage how you are perceived in the organisation.

Networking

Networking is basically getting to know as many people as possible, both in your organisation and outside it. You should not network with any particular goal in mind or looking to gain some advantage — that can come across as pushy and be decidedly counterproductive. Instead, you should simply look to develop relationships and friendships with as many people as possible with no expectations or strings attached. Then, when you are least expecting it, one of these relationships will prove extremely useful. Networking does work — don't miss out.

It's Never Too Late to Change

Career planning will vary greatly from one individual to the next, as some will follow a clear and consistent career path while others discover their true calling later in life. A good example of the latter would be my own career.

After more than 20 years with Unilever, both overseas in Africa and in the UK, I decided to join a highly enlightened strategic consultancy called Marketing Solutions Ltd. This opened up a whole new world to me as I discovered that I enjoyed working with companies, identifying strategic problems and opportunities and then assisting them with implementation plans. After some time there, however, I decided during one of my three-hour thinking sessions that I needed to make some fundamental decisions about my career. I was 53 at the time.

The first decision I made was to visit a health farm on my own for three days of serious and uninterrupted thinking on what I should do. I then came up with three options and wrote out detailed plans for each.

The first option was to stay with the company as an HR director with responsibility for coaching the in-house consultants on how to be more successful. The second option was to leave MSL and form my own consultancy business. This option was attractive but I was concerned about the risk involved, especially at the beginning. I then hit upon a third option which was basically to combine the first two. I would stay on with MSL — guaranteeing a specific fee level from my team over the year — but at the same time be allowed to work with individual clients on my own. When I got home I discussed my plans with my wife, Sue, who as usual made very helpful comments and was very supportive. The Managing Director of MSL agreed to my proposal with enthusiasm and indeed it worked very well for both parties. Eventually I had enough clients whereby I was able to go out on my own entirely.

There are two lessons to be learned from my own career path. First, one should always look for creative and clearly thought-out solutions when considering several options. And second, it is never too late to start up a new career if that's what you really want to do.

Planning Your Career with "Bottle"

As with other aspects of managing discussed in this book, managing your career requires planning and follow-up. It should be part of your three-hour quality thinking sessions and needs to be taken seriously at all times. Many people get stuck in a position, or just float through life without thinking about it, but as you look back on your career you'll be very grateful that you made a special effort to consider all the possibilities — that you managed it with "bottle", which, as we have seen before, is an essential part of achieving success without selling your soul.

Chapter Ten

MANAGING THE BALANCE

Most managers today feel that they are under greater pressure than ever before. Pressure to get results, pressure to impress the right people, pressure to move up the organisation — often pressure merely to survive and hold on to their jobs. It is all very well to say that they shouldn't work until 7.00 or 8.00 every evening, that they shouldn't go in on the weekends and instead spend more time with their families — the sad reality is that many feel that they have to put in that extra effort in the job. Unfortunately, the casualties are all around us: an increase in the divorce rate, alcohol and drug abuse, stress-related illness, and even suicide can be placed at the door of pressures at work.

Many organisations contribute directly to this problem. Accolades and promotions are handed out to those who work long hours, often rewarding such people over more deserving colleagues. People will be lauded for working all weekend or staying in the office until the wee hours of the night in the mistaken belief that such behaviour shows particular devotion and dedication to the job — when in reality it's just a precursor to burn-out.

This chapter looks at why such behaviour is so destructive for managers — and why it harms their organisations as well — and addresses ways to tackle the balance between work life and home life. It compares the typical "extremist" or workaholic manager with the much healthier balanced one, and offers some practical tips on how to put more balance in your life. The chapter looks at the obvious impact company culture has on achieving the balance, and then looks at how more enlightened organisations are taking steps to help their managers to become more balanced. Finally, we look at the importance of balance for becoming a whole manager by putting it into context with the advice given in previous chapters.

The Importance of Balance

When all is said and done, there can be little argument with the observation that "life is for living" and that our goal should be to live it to the full. For many, that will mean a clear focus on their professional lives, but in my experience the truly successful ones are able to keep it in perspective. Having worked with thousands of individuals, both in business and as a consultant, time and time again I have seen the all-round whole manager as the one who gives sustained, ongoing, high-level performance, while the extremists seem to burn themselves out. As we have seen elsewhere in this book, the key to sustained success is prioritising key activities, time management skills, delegating as much as possible, and so forth — it is not about being the last one to leave the office at night.

Workaholics tend to be somewhat out of kilter in general. They often obsess about certain things and miss the bigger picture. They put incredible pressure on themselves, working themselves into the ground in many cases, while their staff members are under-utilised and lacking direction. They are usually poor listeners and overly concerned about what they are going to say next. They are definitely not prioritised, believing that working harder is the only solution. Before long, problems come to the fore — even for the "successful" ones. Relationships deteriorate, health problems arise and performance drops — and the only response they know is to work even harder!

The balanced person will also work very hard, but is more likely to understand the importance of going home at a reasonable hour and taking weekends off. They tend to be more in control of their lives, more amenable to accepting advice and to learning from others. They are relaxed and very positive in their outlook. They are more open-minded and much more likely to see the bigger picture. More importantly, they are also much more likely to be content.

A balanced person also knows himself. I had a certain business friend once who developed health problems and decided that he would not be suited to high-pressured jobs in his company. He thus decided to stay at a level that was well below what he knew he could perform but which also involved less stress. He was nonetheless a highly respected member of the team — indeed, he was often used as an internal consultant by senior managers and the board — and felt that he was in control of his life. Definitely a whole manager.

How to Achieve the Balance

I have had numerous discussions over the years with clients who were concerned about this critical issue of balance. Below are some of the approaches that seemed to work in different areas.

With Children

One client told me that he made a point of setting aside "children time", which typically meant swimming every Saturday morning and help with the homework at least two nights a week. He would also never miss a birthday party or other big event, and was careful to get home in plenty of time to help with any necessary preparations. He was totally dismissive of people who said that they "couldn't take time off". He said that if you are prioritised at all you can make the time for your child's birthday party — and besides, what kind of signal are you sending to the child if you don't bother to turn up for his or her big day? Is your job more important than your family?

With Partner

Again, a balanced manager will set aside time for their partner and be sure not to take anyone for granted. If possible, make one night of the week your night and go to a film or out to dinner or whatever. Take special care in planning anniversaries or birthday celebrations. Be unpredictable — don't allow yourself to get into a rut and just do the same things. The point here is to *value* your partner, and to make sure that he or she *knows* that they are valued. Life is too short not to.

Holidays and Weekends

I have several clients who book their annual holidays a full 12 months in advance. This means that they have a definite break to look forward to and that it is as important in the diary as any other business event. Whenever possible, I advise clients to take two breaks per year, even if they need to be shorter ones, so that they have time to recharge their batteries and keep things in perspective.

I have another client who schedules special "*a deux*" weekends to go away somewhere nice with his wife. Again, this gives them something to look forward to and lets his wife know she is appreciated.

Yet another client sets aside "do nothing" weekends where she doesn't allow anything to be scheduled whatsoever. This ensures that she can spend time with her family, as well as giving her time to think and contemplate.

Sports, Hobbies, etc.

There are obviously numerous activities that can provide relaxation and enjoyment away from the workplace — although in some cases the obsession of work is simply transferred to an obsession with golf or tennis or something else. And the problem of the "golf widow" — the wife whose husband is at work all week and on the golf course all weekend — is a real one. A bit of consideration and common sense will solve the problem, however. Just be sure that your sport or hobby is providing a healthy outlet and that — as always! — you approach it with a sense of balance.

No doubt the above advice sounds fairly basic and even mundane. For many, simple common sense tells them that they need to spend time away from work. And yet it is remarkable how many fail to do so, how many simply "don't have the time". Those are the people who need to step back and take a look at their lives — before the ulcer hits!

Balance and "Bottle"

Much has been said earlier about the importance of "bottle" in business — of managing with integrity and being true to yourself. The same is true in your home life and in finding the balance.

Many people use the pressures of work as an excuse to avoid responsibilities at home. They tell their partners — and possibly themselves as well — that they were simply "too busy" to show up at Johnny's party, or that they missed dinner at home because they were "swamped" at the office, or that it was because they were under "so much pressure" that they forgot their anniversary. Utter nonsense — and cowardly as well.

You need to have the "bottle" to do the right thing by your partner or family, and if you honestly can't, then you need to have the "bottle" to make it up to them somehow. And if this happens often, you need to take a hard look at how you are managing your time and priorities.

A young woman I know, who had a young child, was doing excellent work as an account manager. Often she would still be in the office at ten o'clock at night, however, putting the finishing touches to a project or catching up on her correspondence. When this came to her boss's attention, he asked her why it was necessary to work so late since the other managers were able to cope during regular business hours. The sad reply was that she preferred the office to the more mundane and boring work of being a mother to her child.

Simply stated, this woman was not managing with "bottle". She was on a bit of an ego trip and felt that her work life was more important than her home life. She was not thinking about her child, her partner, or her home life. She did not realise that she had other things to work at besides those in the office. She was fortunate that her boss had the good sense to confront her about it and to impress upon her the need to work on the balance. And, obviously, there are many men in a similar situation.

Company Culture

Most of what has been written so far on balance has focused on what individual managers should be doing. The fact remains, however, that each individual manager is part of an organisation and each organisation will have its own culture. For example, in some companies it would be seriously frowned upon if someone were to take a three-week holiday — even if it had been approved by the individual's immediate boss and would not cause hardship to others. Similarly, as noted earlier, the culture of many companies is to reward — even to expect — working late and on the weekends.

But suppose you resolve to inject some balance into your life, to go home at a reasonable hour and spend more time with your family, and your boss is simply not interested in this whole idea of balance. Suppose your boss is only interested in bottom line results like exceeding sales targets, or worse yet, was obsessed that his team should be seen to be "working their butts off" at all times. What then?

Clearly you would need to step lightly here, but I would advise you to look back on the advice given in the chapter on "Managing Upwards" and indeed in other chapters as well. You would need to work hard on communicating with your boss, and in particular on understanding on what basis your work would be measured. You need to have regular discussions about your top priorities and the progress being made on them. You need to explain that you are devoted to your work and to the success of the company, but that you also have a family life that is important. The key would be to focus on the quality of your work, the actual results you are achieving, rather than on the extra hours. And at the end of the day, you should have the "bottle" to go home at your usual time. If your boss should confront you about why you are leaving "early", you would then need to have another discussion about your top priorities and your boss's expectations.

Fortunately, there are signs that such bosses will some day become a minority. While some organisations still cling to the notion that work life and personal life are competing priorities and that a gain in one means a loss in the other, an increasing number of companies are trying to develop a culture where managers and employees collaborate to achieve work and personal objectives to everyone's benefit. This makes sense since employees with outside interests tend to be well-rounded, healthy and content, which obviously makes them more effective employees.

The evidence so far is that managers who are acting on these principles have discovered that conflicts between work and personal priorities can actually act as catalysts for discovering more efficient ways to work. For example, I heard of one manager who was able to work with his staff to find a way to deal with increased workload while actually granting the staff more concentrated time off.

As noted elsewhere in the book, people are one of the most important resources in any organisation and new approaches like the above will become increasingly important in retaining high quality workers.

Putting It All Together

Many of the issues addressed in this book are appropriate for helping you to obtain balance in your life. Indeed, the primary message of the book is that with careful planning and foresight, anyone can be successful both at work and at home. As a way of concluding both this chapter and the book as a whole, I now list my ten steps to business and personal success, which can be a useful summary of the previous chapters. I hope you will find this advice very helpful as you make the journey through your career and life. I wish you the best of luck!

Peter Bolt's Ten Steps for Achieving Success Without Selling Your Soul

1. **You can't manage others if you can't manage yourself**. Realise that you are in charge of your life and that it's up to you to make a success of it. Learn

the value of being well prepared at all times, under-stand your priorities, welcome accountability and even adversity, and develop and maintain a positive attitude.

2. **Time is your most valuable asset — use it wisely**. Don't be one of those managers who are slaves of time. Develop time management strategies that will ensure that you are on top of both work and home time pressures. And above all, remember to schedule your regular three-hour thinking sessions so that you allow yourself quality time to think through the big issues.

3. **Perception is reality**. How you are perceived by your superiors, peers and team members is of critical importance to your success in your organisation. Be sure you are aware of how others see you — even if you think it unfair or inaccurate — so that you can take steps to correct it.

4. **Be a manager who gets things done**. Success will depend on getting things done so you need to develop a mindset and approach that is results-oriented. Plan your activities carefully, and then find ways to ensure that they happen on time and as planned.

5. **Perfect the art of delegation**. Delegating work to others is a key component of successful management — and not delegating often leads to disaster.

Delegating does not mean abdicating responsibility, but rather developing your team to their full potential and allowing you to concentrate on matters of importance. Successful delegation has an impact on time management, leadership, getting things done, managing the balance and much more — work on it today!

6. **Be a manager that inspires others**. Being a leader that others want to follow is another key component of being a successful manager. Remember at all times that people are your most valuable resource and that it is up to you to get the most out of them you can. Learn to manage fairly but firmly, to be a mentor and a coach but also disciplinarian as needed, and to set a good example in both what you say and what you do.

7. **Learn how to manage upwards, downwards and sideways in the organisation**. Being a successful manager is about more than just leading your team. You must also understand how to manage upwards, so that you develop a strong sustained relationship with your boss, and also to manage sideways so that you work well with your peers. This requires strong communication skills, as well as good interpersonal skills that help you to understand and respond to the needs of others.

8. **Actively manage your career**. To be successful you need to try to understand at all times where you've been and where you're going. Don't be someone who just floats through life and takes things as they come. Be flexible and open to new challenges, but also take time to reflect on the choices before you. Know your strengths and weaknesses, be true to yourself, and then have the "bottle" to go for it.

9. **Act with integrity at all times — be a manager (and person) with "bottle"**. Achieving success by less than honourable means is a hollow victory. Cutting corners, stabbing colleagues in the back, being disloyal to your boss or organisation, are all examples of managers lacking integrity. When faced with an ethical dilemma, consider the options and repercussions carefully, and then be true to yourself. You have to be able to live with your actions. This also pertains to your home life. Be someone who has the "bottle" to place your family life before your work life, to appreciate your partner and to spend time with your children. You won't regret it.

10. **Find the balance**. Life is short and it's up to you to make the most of your time on the planet. If you find that you are under pressure at work, that you are working many more hours than you should be, that your mental and physical well-being are at risk, then STOP — think about what you are doing and what you want out of life. And then take whatever

steps are needed to change things. If you do, you may find what you have been missing all these years.

Let Me Hear from You

As mentioned in the preface, I have been fascinated for years with the problem of how to be a success in business without sacrificing your integrity, your home life or your self-respect. In numerous seminars and one-on-one coaching sessions I have been moved by how people struggle with this issue and by their heartfelt appreciation and gratitude upon hearing this simple message: you don't have to sacrifice your soul to get ahead. I am grateful to all who have shared their experiences with me in the past, and I would be equally grateful to any readers who wrote to tell me about your attempts at finding the balance. I promise to respect your confidentiality but, with permission, I would hope to share your experiences in future editions of this book. I look forward to hearing from you.

Peter Bolt
The Bolt Consultancy
12 Devonhurst Place
Chiswick, London W4 4JB
Fax: 0181 747 0461

INDEX